Helaine Becker

**Cover and illustrations
by Joanna Sevilla**

Scholastic Canada Ltd.
Toronto New York London Auckland Sydney
Mexico City New Delhi Hong Kong Buenos Aires

For my mom, who taught me ALL about stress 😝

—HB

Scholastic Canada Ltd.
604 King Street West, Toronto, Ontario M5V 1E1, Canada

Scholastic Inc.
557 Broadway, New York, NY 10012, USA

Scholastic Australia Pty Limited
PO Box 579, Gosford, NSW 2250, Australia

Scholastic New Zealand Limited
Private Bag 94407, Botany, Manukau 2163, New Zealand

Scholastic Children's Books
Euston House, 24 Eversholt Street, London NW1 1DB, UK

www.scholastic.ca

Thank you to Dr. Tasha Brown, clinical psychologist, for providing an expert review of this book.

Library and Archives Canada Cataloguing in Publication
Title: So long, stress! / Helaine Becker ; original illustrations by Joanna Sevilla.
Names: Becker, Helaine, author. | Sevilla, Joanna, illustrator.
Identifiers: Canadiana 20220407371 | ISBN 9781443187701 (softcover)
Subjects: LCSH: Stress management for children—Juvenile literature. | LCSH: Stress in children — Juvenile literature. | LCSH: Stress management—Juvenile literature. | LCSH: Stress (Psychology) — Juvenile literature.
Classification: LCC RA785 .B43 2023 | DDC j155.9/042—dc23

Illustrations on pages 6-7, 9, 15, 16-17, 29, 35, 41, 43, 45, 46-47, 53, 54, 55, 57, 65, 67, 69, 72-73, 76, 79, 80, 83, 84, 87, 88, 91, 106, 108, 114-115, 119, 121, 122, 127, 130, 134, 137, 142, 144-145, 147 by Joanna Sevilla.

Stock photos © Shutterstock.com.

Text copyright © 2023 by Helaine Becker.
Illustrations copyright © 2023 by Scholastic Canada Ltd.
All rights reserved.

No part of this publication may be reproduced or stored in a retrieval system, or transmitted in any form or by any means, electronic, mechanical, recording, or otherwise, without written permission of the publisher, Scholastic Canada Ltd., 604 King Street West, Toronto, Ontario M5V 1E1, Canada. In the case of photocopying or other reprographic copying, a licence must be obtained from Access Copyright (Canadian Copyright Licensing Agency), www.accesscopyright.ca or 1-800-893-5777.

6 5 4 3 2 1 Printed in China 62 23 24 25 26 27

Contents

Stress Happens! 4
Part 1: What Is Stress? 6
- How Does Stress Work? 8
- How Does Stress Feel? 10
- Too Much Stress! 12
- Tune In to Your Signs of Stress 14

Part 2: Developing Stress-Fighting Habits 16
- Get Organized 18
- Develop a Growth Mindset 24
- Practise Active Relaxation 30
- Calm Your Mind 38
- Take Time to Notice 44
- Move Your Body 52
- Fuel Your Body 58
- Rest Your Body 64

Part 3: Taking Care of Emotions 72
- Connect with Your Emotions 74
- Make Personal Connections 82
- Practise Self-Care! 92
- Channel Your Creative Side 102

Part 4: Tackling Stressful Situations 114
- When You're Feeling Overwhelmed 116
- Making Decisions 126
- Dealing with Conflict 138

Part 5: When to Get Help 144
Resources 149
Index 151

Stress Happens!

You know in your gut what stress is. You've felt it if you've ever had a disagreement with a friend, bickered with a parent about household chores or had to juggle piano practice, soccer drills, school work and time with your friends. It can feel like you're in a stress pressure cooker.

I've felt all of those things, especially during my teen years, when I was plagued by anxiety and riddled with self-doubt. In those days, the adults in my life didn't always get that kids' stress is real stress. We were told to "have a stiff upper lip" or "get a grip."

Thankfully times have changed. More adults understand that stress can affect anyone, no matter how old we are, and that learning how to manage that stress is especially important when we are young.

This book is the resource I would have loved to have had in my middle school years. It offers a wide variety of strategies to help you cope with daily stress. I use many of these strategies now, and they work for me.

Not all of the tips you'll find in this book will work for you, but many will! The trick is to create your own personal stress-reduction "tool kit" full of strategies you can rely on again and again.

This book is divided into sections to help you find the information you need when you need it. I hope you find it both useful and fun!

In **PART 1** you'll find out why you need stress for survival and how much stress is too much.

PART 2 is all about developing habits to help you prevent and combat stress. Taking care of your body, strengthening your mind and practising relaxation will make you better at dealing with stress.

PART 3 dives into your social and emotional life. Strategies in this section deal with figuring out your feelings, learning how to manage and share your emotions effectively, maintaining healthy relationships and expressing yourself through creativity.

PART 4 is all about the moment of crisis — when you find yourself in a stressful situation. This section provides easy-to-use strategies for when you feel overwhelmed or under severe pressure, to help you make tough decisions and to deal with conflicts that inevitably arise with your classmates, friends and family.

Sometimes, handling stress is just too hard to do on your own. You don't have to. **PART 5** provides guidance for how to get help when you need it.

Try a few strategies from each of the categories in parts 2 and 3. Before long you'll have a customized stress-beating tool kit you can draw from to help you feel calm and strong every day — and during those particularly stressful moments. Soon you'll be able to say, **"SO LONG, STRESS!"**

All the best,

Helaine

PART 1

Stress is the way the body reacts to challenges, both good and bad. It's a signal that you need to make a change. Stress isn't good or bad. It's simply a call to action.

The body releases hormones called adrenalin (or epinephrine) and cortisol to prepare your body to respond to danger and take action. How you react to those signals is up to you.

Stress is a natural, even necessary part of life. But too much stress can sometimes give way to *distress*.

Distress is what people are usually talking about when they say "I feel stressed." When you're distressed, you might feel scared, upset, overwhelmed or anxious. If they go on for a long period of time, feelings of distress can even make you physically sick.

Learning to recognize what causes you distress and managing your responses to it are important for helping you stay happy and healthy.

How Does Stress Work?

When you find yourself in a stressful situation, your body quickly begins to respond. This reaction is known as the stress response. You might also hear it referred to as an adrenalin rush or the fight-or-flight reaction.

Your brain sends chemical signals to the adrenal glands, where the hormones adrenalin and cortisol are produced. Then these hormones circulate through your body, affecting most of your organs.

Your heart and lungs send extra blood and oxygen to your brain and limbs. Your senses of sight and hearing sharpen. Stored glucose (sugar) and fats flood into your bloodstream, fuelling a burst of energy. Your muscles tense to guard against injury and/or to prepare for escape.

All of these adaptations have evolved to help you react faster to a threat. You can see and hear better, think faster and run away with superhuman speed, or fight with superhuman strength if you have to.

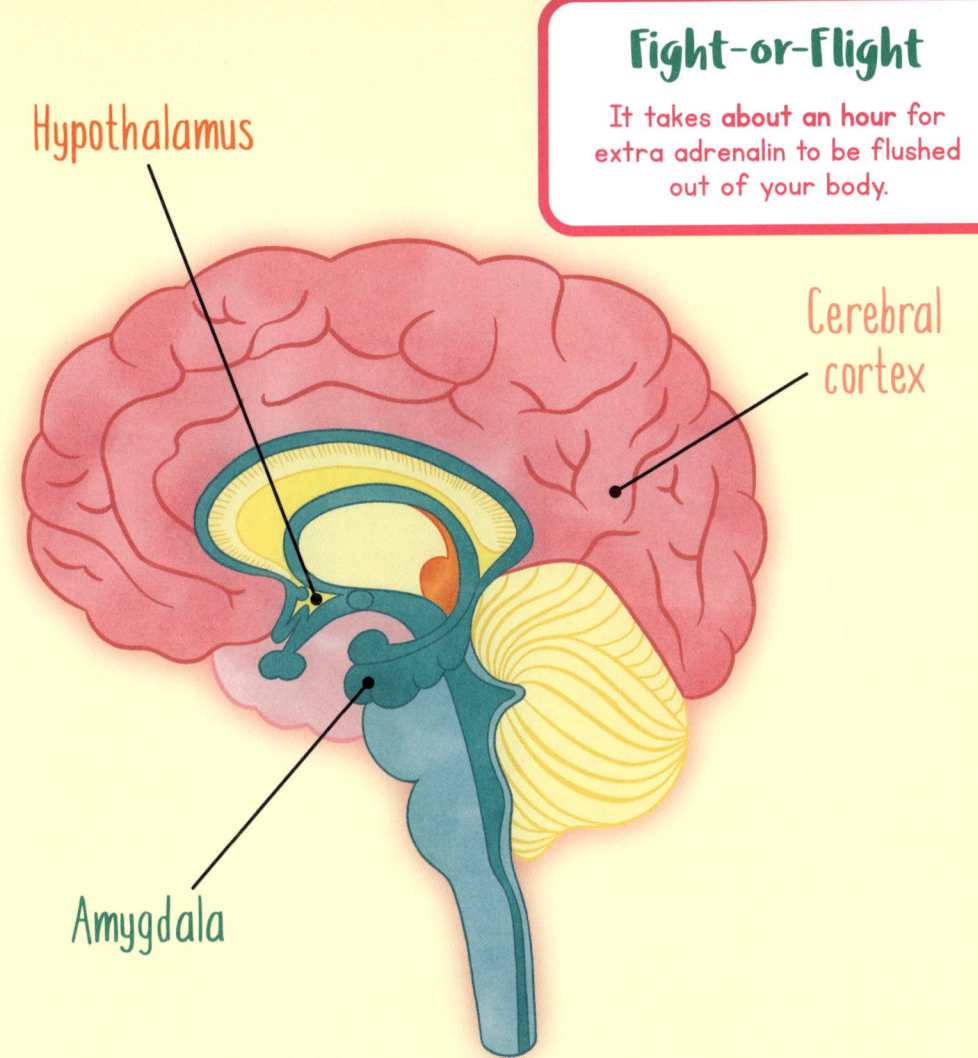

Fight-or-Flight

It takes **about an hour** for extra adrenalin to be flushed out of your body.

The cerebral cortex is the part of the brain where thinking and decision making happens. The amygdala is where we process emotions. When triggered by a stressful event or thought, the amygdala sends a chemical message to the hypothalamus, the brain's "mission control center." When it kicks into gear, it triggers the stress response.

Because the stress response bypasses the cerebral cortex, you can react more quickly than usual without hesitating or overthinking. For the same reason, people often find it difficult to think clearly or rationally while under stress.

How Does Stress Feel?

Everyone experiences stress differently. Learning to recognize what stress feels like to you will help you manage how you respond.

Think back on a stressful situation and take note of how your body felt at the time. Here are some common stress reactions. Do any of them seem familiar?

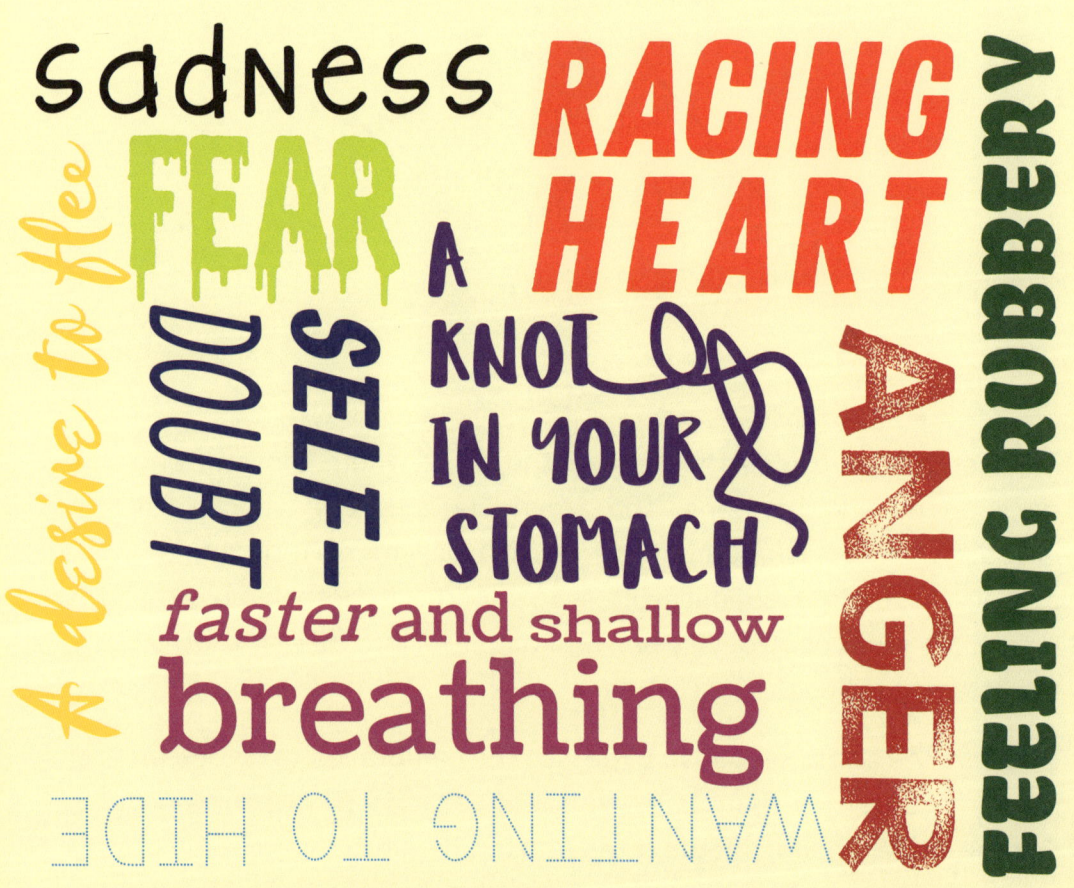

sadness • RACING HEART • FEAR • A desire to flee • SELF-DOUBT • A knot in your stomach • ANGER • FEELING RUBBERY • faster and shallow breathing • WANTING TO HIDE

What Stresses You Out?

Just as everyone differs in how they react to stress, what triggers stress also varies from person to person, and from time to time.

Stress can come from many sources: your family, friends and acquaintances, school, the environment and yourself! Being aware of the people and situations that trigger the stress response for you will help you prepare to face stressful times more effectively.

To figure out your top tension sources, try this visualization exercise. Imagine a typical day, beginning with waking up, getting dressed, heading off to school. Picture each "scene" in your mental movie as vividly as you can. As you scroll through each scene, pay careful attention to any physical reactions in your body. Does your stomach knot or your heart start to race? These are clues that something about that part of your day is stressful to you.

Take a Stress Self-Check

Give yourself a stress self-check a few times each day. Mentally scan your body for symptoms of stress. For example, are you clenching your teeth? If so, loosen up and take a deep, relaxing breath. Getting into the self-check habit will help you recognize situations or activities that cause you distress.

Too MUCH Stress!

The stress response has evolved over millions of years to help us avoid life-threatening situations. But what about when we face non-life-threatening stressors, like a big test or auditioning for the school play? Can we react with a stress response that's less, well, *stressful*?

Unfortunately, no. Our brains and bodies react to all stressors, no matter how minor, as if they were furious, charging rhinos.

When life is full of stressors (big or small), it can feel like your body is in a semi-permanent state of high alert. Elevated levels of adrenalin and cortisol over a long period of time can lead to a condition called chronic stress.

Chronic stress keeps you from feeling your best. It affects how you sleep, eat and even go to the bathroom. Your mood, your energy level and your ability to focus can all be affected by chronic stress.

Left unchecked, chronic stress can lead to serious health issues. So learning how to recognize and manage everyday stress will keep you healthier today and every day.

Know YOUR Stress Triggers

Think of recent times when you've felt an adrenalin rush. What were you doing? How did you feel? And what did you DO in response? Make a list of the sensations you experienced and places or times you have felt this way so you can start to be more aware of what triggers your distress.

Tune In to Your Signs of Stress

People react to stress differently, but most people respond to stress in broadly similar ways.

Some signs of stress are clear — the racing heart, the sweaty palms. Others are less obvious. These can include:

- Having trouble falling asleep
- Your stomach knotting up
- Losing your temper
- Fidgeting
- Fretting over every little thing
- Losing your appetite
- Feeling sluggish or listless

Keep in mind that everyone occasionally has trouble sleeping or gets cranky or irritable. But if "occasionally" turns into "frequently," stress might be the underlying cause.

Coping Strategies

Any action you take to relieve stress and help yourself feel better is called a coping strategy. Taking a hot bath, going for a bike ride with a friend and writing in your journal are all examples of effective coping strategies.

Not all coping strategies, however, are positive. Negative strategies, like staying in bed and hiding under the covers, might give you relief in the short run. In the long run, though, they can make stress worse. A lot worse.

PART 2

Stress may be a normal part of life, but we don't need to let it run riot through our day or control us. There are many different techniques for managing stress. Some of them will help you keep your cool in the moment. Others can help you protect yourself from getting stressed in the first place. Still others will help you recover faster from stressful incidents.

You already know that if you want to improve your time in the hundred-metre dash or become a champion speller, you have to work on your skills ahead of time. Learning how to manage stress also takes practice.

Get *ready* by deciding which stress busters might work for you. *Set* yourself up for success by working on them every day. You'll be honing your skills so you'll have them at your fingertips when you need them. You'll be in top stress-busting form when it's time to *go*!

Get Organized

You might have heard the expression "an ounce of prevention is worth a pound of cure." It means that it's easier to prevent a problem than to fix it. The same idea holds true for stress. Luckily, many everyday stressors are a snap to short-circuit using common organizational techniques and tools.

In this section, you'll find suggestions for how to use everyday organizing techniques to help manage and prevent stress. Putting them to work today can make you feel calmer and more in control right away. It will also help you avoid a lot of stress-inducing frustration tomorrow.

Keep a Calendar

Homework due dates, birthdays, softball team practices . . . all of these events are date-driven, meaning they happen at specific times. The busier your life becomes, the easier it is to forget those key dates.

To keep date-driven stress from derailing your day, set up — and use — a calendar daily. Whether it's pinned to your wall, in your school agenda or on your phone, your calendar will "remember" upcoming events so you don't have to.

Calendar quick tips:

- Keep your calendar where it's easy to see.

- Check it daily. Calendars aren't much use if you mark things down on them but never check them!

- Set off important dates by outlining them with colourful markers or highlighting them with stickers.

- If you are using a calendar app on a phone or computer, set up reminders so you get notified ahead of time for important events.

Put Everything in Its Place

You *know* you brought that book home from school. And where is that water bottle you took to dance class yesterday? They've got to be here . . . somewhere . . .

Do you waste a lot of time looking for missing stuff? If so, you know how the endless searching chips away at your free time while it piles on stress and frustration.

Making sure you can find any item you need is therefore a genius way to prevent stress. The smaller your space, the more important keeping it organized becomes.

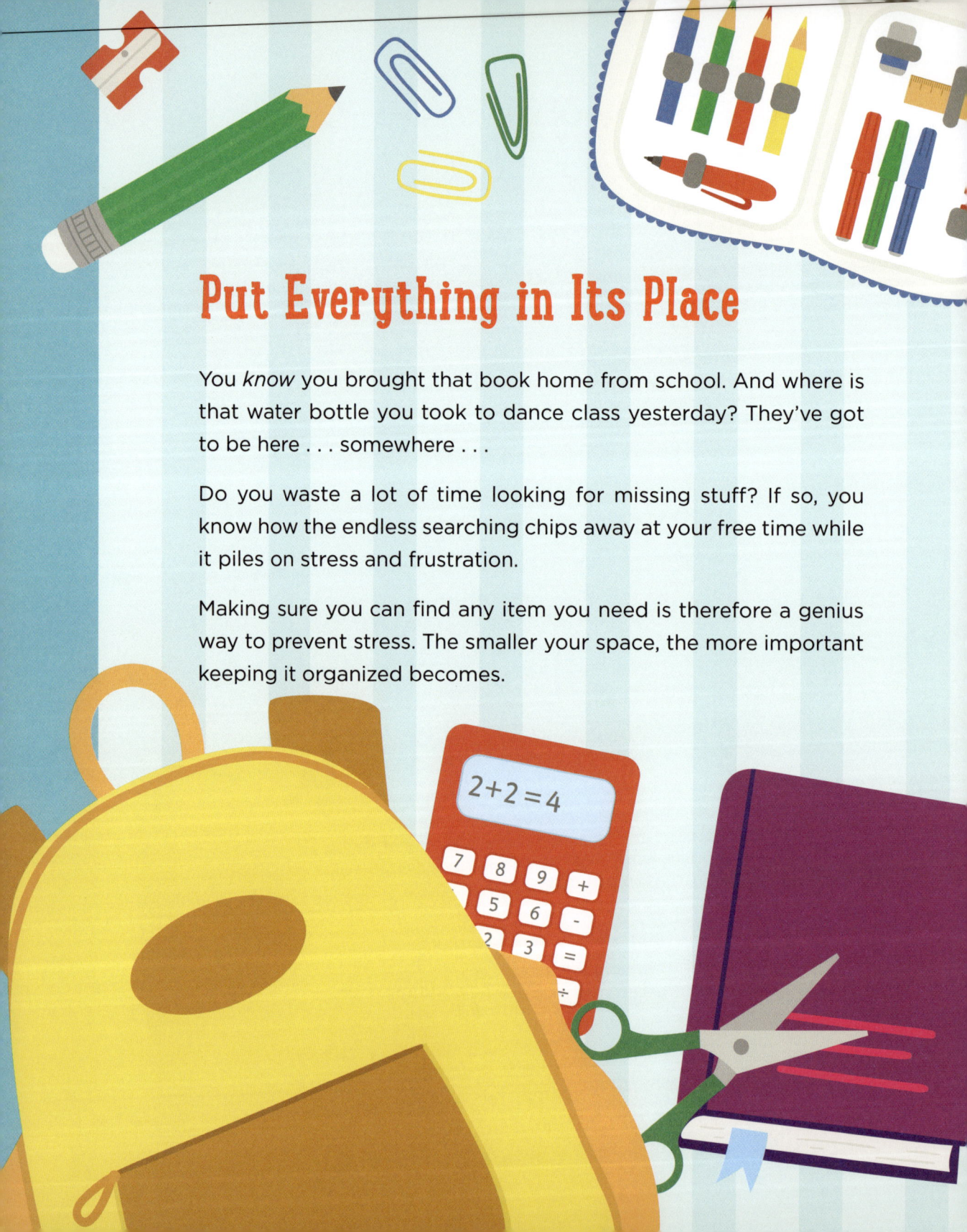

Consider some or all of these time-tested tricks:

MAKE IT A RAINBOW!
Group similarly coloured items together. It will be faster and easier to find what you want when you want it, and easier to tidy up. Your rainbow will look nice too!

THINK FUNCTION FIRST!
Group items that perform the same task — all your pencils, for example — together. Put the erasers nearby, but in their own container.

HOME SWEET HOME!
Create homes for stuff you use every day and put your things in their place every night. You'll never waste time and energy hunting for things when you need them!

LABEL EVERYTHING!
Labels are your friend. Whether you use premade stickers or tags you've created with scrap paper and markers, labels help you find stuff fast.

THINK VERTICALLY!
Got a messy stack of homework assignments spilling across your desk? Store those loose sheets of paper upright in a binder or an empty cereal box! Separate them by subject with a coloured sheet of paper or a book.

VISIBILITY IS KEY!
Organizers you hang up or lean against a wall, like pegboards and corkboards, are useful for keeping your stuff easily accessible and visible, without cluttering up your desk or dresser.

DIVIDE TO CONQUER!
Drawers all a-jumble? Use dividers to help keep individual items separate so they are easier to find. You can make your own using a piece of corrugated cardboard cut to size.

NEST IT.
Pencils, rulers and erasers are all separate items. But they can be grouped together under "school supplies." Nest each separate group within a larger organizer, like a drawer or storage box.

Corral the Clutter

Are yesterday's clothes and towels strewn across your bedroom floor? Is your school desk or locker jammed with old assignments, book bags and gym shoes you never use?

Most of us have *waaaaay* more stuff than we need. The result is clutter, clutter and more clutter.

Clutter isn't just a minor irritation, though. It creates a kind of visual chaos that contributes to stress. Numerous scientific studies have shown that living or working in a cluttered environment triggers the stress response. Cluttered spaces also make it harder to focus, and they impair your memory and ability to sleep.

Minimize clutter by taking these simple steps:

SORT your stuff into categories.

TOSS or give away what you don't need or want.

STORE related items in neat, labelled containers.

KEEP shelves, desktops and cupboards neat and free of extraneous items.

Create a Vision Board

Reminding yourself regularly of your goals and dreams helps you stay on track and motivated. With a vision board, you can see your goals as well as the path to make them happen.

You can make your own vision board out of practically anything — poster board, corkboard, even a sheet of cardboard. And you can put it anywhere you will see it regularly.

Use your vision board as a home for pictures, phrases and ideas that inspire you. If you dream of becoming a world traveller, include photos of places you want to go, bubble-letter ways to say hello in different languages and add a packing list for your dream vacation. There are no rules — include whatever inspires you.

Vision boards are inspirational, but they are also practical. If you're feeling overwhelmed or distracted by all the competing demands of life, a quick peek at your vision board can remind you of what's important to you. Vision boards can also act as a place of refuge. You can lose yourself in them, imagining the wonderful future that you are creating!

De-clutter Tip

Make your bed if you plan to hang out or do homework in your room after school. It's an instant clutter crusher.

Develop a Growth Mindset

In this section, you'll learn how to cultivate a healthy, productive way of thinking called the growth mindset. It's more than a positive attitude — the growth mindset is rooted in the idea that *everyone* can learn, change and grow. An individual's characteristics and abilities are not fixed but can be improved with effort, training and experience.

As you cultivate your growth mindset, you'll get better at seeing that challenges are opportunities. You'll be better at coming up with plans to achieve your goals, and not get in your own way by focusing on perceived weaknesses or obstacles. And when you try new things or take on challenges, you'll feel less stressed and more capable, no matter the outcome.

Celebrate Your ... Weaknesses?

Of course you have weaknesses. Everyone does. But they don't have to make you feel bad.

Instead of dwelling on your shortcomings, focus on ways to overcome them.

The first step is to be honest with yourself: acknowledge your weaknesses. Okay, so maybe you're not the best tuba player in the school band. It's not the end of the world. And it's not a fact that's etched in stone either. Remember that you have the power to change your habits and abilities. Your lousy tuba technique is actually a perfect opportunity for growth!

Once you've rejigged your perspective, you can take real, positive action. How can you improve your horn-playing skills? You might create a practice schedule and stick to it, or get tips from your music teachers and other kids in the band. Or maybe you'll try breathing exercises to improve your lung power.

It will take plenty of work and commitment to put more *oomph* into your *oompah-pah*, but you can definitely do it if you put your heart and soul into it. And even if you don't ever become a tuba star, you'll be happier about blowing your own horn.

> Your weaknesses are simply strengths waiting to be unleashed.

Growing a Growth Mindset

Think of your thoughts as seeds. Depending on which seeds you plant, you'll wind up with different sorts of crops.

Optimistic thought-seeds ("I can do this!") grow joy and opportunity. Negative ones ("I'm a failure") breed stress and make it harder to connect with others and achieve your goals.

You can prepare your mental soil to encourage the growth of the most helpful, positive thoughts. Through practice, you can also learn how to weed out the stress-causing ones whenever they crop up. The result — a bountiful harvest of happiness.

Make a List!

Make a list of your positive qualities. They can be serious or wacky. Post it where you can see it and add new examples as you think of them.

Just Add Fertilizer

To grow a healthier, stress-beating attitude:

- Embrace new challenges as opportunities. Even if you don't succeed the first time, you will learn from the experience and improve.

- Do you dream of executing a flawless, gold medal–winning triple axel? Doing so will mean you'll flub your axels hundreds, even thousands of times. Remember that failure is the first, necessary step on the road to success. You can't succeed if you never fail.

- Keep in mind that criticism isn't always meant as a put-down. When it comes from a caring friend, parent or teacher, it's actually a hand-up — a suggestion for helping you become your best self.

Mistakes Are AMAZING!

Every time you make a mistake, your brain strengthens the connections on the path to a right answer. Mistakes pave the way to success!

Conquer the Learning Curve

Irish dancing? Stop-frame animation? Stitching a quilt? Whatever new activity catches your fancy, mastering it won't be a walk in the park. That's because learning a new skill is like climbing a big hill.

When you start out, you're full of enthusiasm and energy, right? But as you continue, the hill gets steeper. The climb gets tougher. You grow tired and frustrated. But there's still so far to go! *Arrrgh!* You're seriously tempted to call it quits.

This is the point when many people do quit. Like the steepest part of a mountain trail, the steepest part of the "learning curve" is really, really tough going. For everybody.

But if you stick it out, you know what will happen? The path to the summit levels out. It gets easier to climb. The terrain opens up, giving you an inspiring glimpse of the summit.

Before you know it, you'll reach the top. And when you get there, you'll be Irish dancing like a born Dubliner.

Be Willing to Bend

When you're climbing that mountain, you won't be able to see what lies beyond every hairpin turn. The peak itself might be hidden behind clouds.

Hikers know they can't plan for every single detail of their trip. They need to be flexible, able to respond to changes on the fly. When they stumble across fallen branches or a grazing doe, they are ready to react appropriately.

The same thing goes for you, in everyday life. You can't know exactly what's going to happen next, all the time. Nor can you be prepared for every possible outcome.

That's why the ability to bend and go with the flow is so helpful for beating stress. When you are willing to let go of rigid plans and trust yourself, you worry less and enjoy yourself more.

Practise Active Relaxation

In much the same way that stress is both a feeling and a physical reaction (see "How Does Stress Work?" on page 8), so is relaxation. When you feel relaxed, it is thanks to a variety of feel-good hormones circulating in your bloodstream. Those hormones relax your muscles, slow your breathing and heart rate, and make you feel sleepy or give you a sense of peace and well-being.

All together, these reactions are called the relaxation response. Most of us just call it feeling great.

The relaxation response occurs naturally, like after you exercise or when you're kicking back with a good book. But you can also *consciously control* it, setting those feel-good hormones flowing through your body when you need 'em.

The various techniques described in this section are proven to trigger the relaxation response. Daily practice will help you feel calmer and clearer every day. You'll sleep better too.

When you find yourself in a stressful situation, you can use your relaxation skills to take the tension down a notch. You'll recover faster from an adrenalin rush too.

The Relaxation Response

The relaxation response is the opposite of the stress response. The neurotransmitter acetylcholine shuts down the release of adrenalin and cortisol. This helps the body recover after a stressful incident. It also keeps your body's processes working efficiently so you feel your best.

Control Your Breath

When you are tense or nervous, your breathing automatically speeds up and becomes shallower.

When you relax, your breathing automatically slows down and becomes deeper.

While the relaxation response can trigger changes in how you breathe, changing how you breathe can also trigger the relaxation response! So when you take conscious control of it, your breath can be a powerful stress-reducer.

Because it's not something we are used to doing, conscious breathing is not easy. Like any skill, the more you practise, the better you get at it.

Box Breathing

Box breathing is a simple technique to slow your breathing. It is frequently used by first responders to help them stay calm during a crisis. It's called box or four-square breathing because when you do it, each of the four "sides" of your complete cycle of breath are exactly the same length.

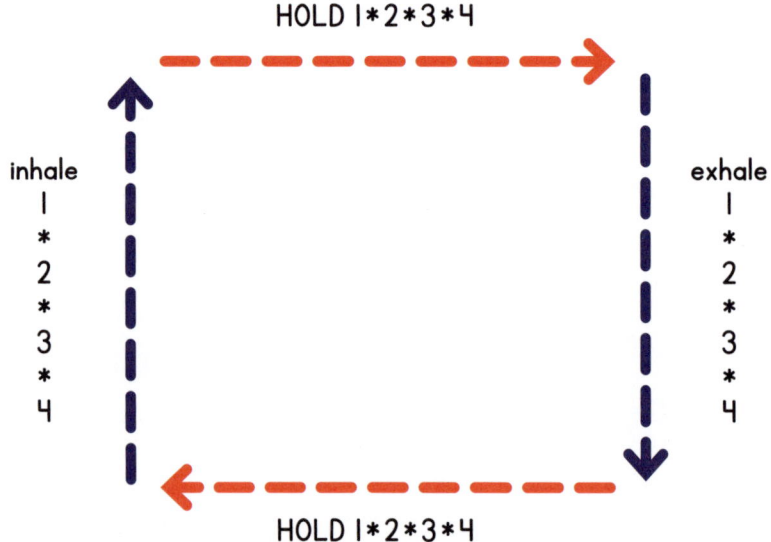

1. Begin by exhaling for a count of four.

2. Hold for a count of four.

3. Inhale for a count of four.

4. Hold for a count of four.

For best results, repeat the box four times.

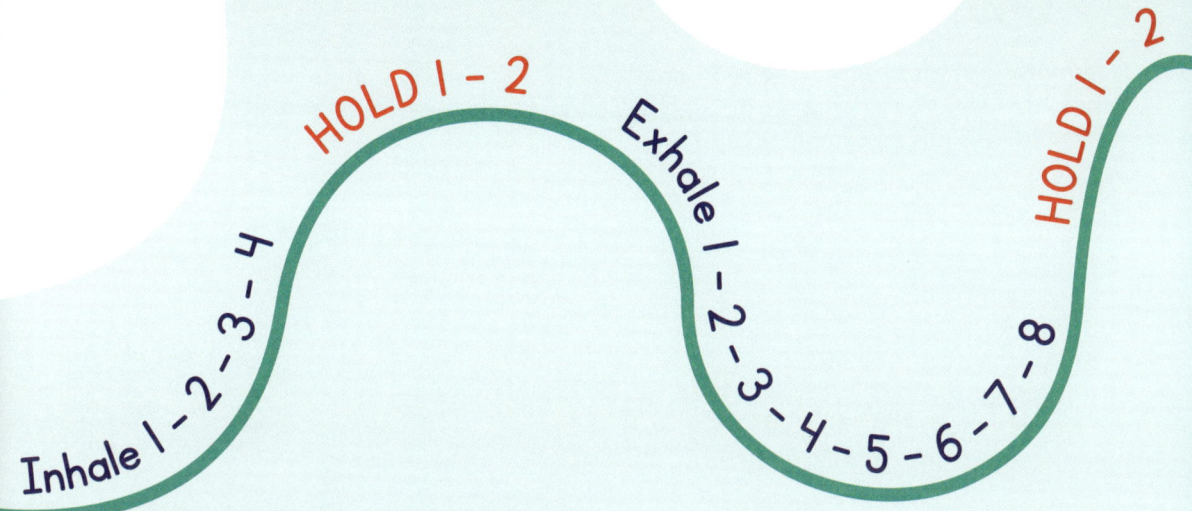

Paced Breathing

Are you more of an out-of-the-box kind of person? This breathing technique might be the right one for you. You can vary the length of each step to suit your preferences; the key is that the time you spend exhaling is roughly double the time spent inhaling.

1. Breathe in for a count of four.

2. Hold your breath for a count of two.

3. Let the breath out slowly, for a count of eight.

4. Hold again for a count of two.

5. Repeat six to twelve times.

Focus on Each Breath

Add more *oomph* to any breathing exercise by really focusing on each breath, shutting out other thoughts and sensations.

The Cooling Breath

This breathing technique, called sitali pranayama in Sanskrit, comes from the practice of yoga. It makes keeping your cool fun.

1. Sit somewhere comfy, keeping your back straight.

2. Lower your chin. Stick out your tongue and roll it, if you can, into the shape of a hot dog bun.

3. With your tongue still out, breathe in through your mouth. At the same time, slowly lift your chin until you're gazing at the ceiling. You might feel cool air flowing over your tongue.

4. To exhale, pull in your tongue, close your mouth, lower your chin and exhale through your nose.

5. Repeat eight to twelve times.

Alternate Nostril Breathing

This breath-control technique is especially useful before heading into a stressful situation, like a test or a performance — when you want to feel relaxed and alert.

1. Press your right thumb over your right nostril to close it.
2. Inhale deeply through your left nostril.
3. When you're ready to exhale, pinch the left nostril and uncover your right nostril.
4. Exhale through the right nostril.
5. Inhale through the right nostril.
6. Pinch the right nostril closed and open the left nostril.
7. Exhale through the left nostril.
8. Repeat eight to twelve times.

Mindful Breathing

For this five-minute breath-control technique, you'll need a stopwatch or clock with a second hand.

Minute 1:

Get comfy and breathe normally. Count the number of times you inhale and exhale (1 inhale + 1 exhale = 1 breath).

Minutes 2 and 3:

Continue breathing normally. Take notice: Is your breathing slowing down, without your even trying?

Minutes 4 and 5:

Consciously slow your breathing.

Ocean Breathing

Close your eyes. Pay close attention to the sound of your breath. Does it remind you of the *swoosh*, *swoosh*, *swoosh* of waves breaking and receding?

Ebb and flow, back and forth, up and down . . . your lungs are like miniature, self-contained oceans. And like the endless, restless sea, they're a source of power. You tap into that natural energy when you pay attention to the ins and outs of your breath.

As long as you live, your breath will sustain you. Honour it. Let it lift you up. Let it bring you peace.

Calm Your Mind

If you've ever spent a restless night tossing and turning, you know that sometimes your body can feel relaxed while your mind still races wildly. You also know that a busy brain that won't quiet down can keep you on edge 24-7. That might leave you feeling burnt-out.

But you have the ability to rein in racing thoughts. The tips in this section show you how to use your natural talents, like keen hearing or skills of proprioception (knowing where your body is in space), to create mental calm. Combined with breathing exercises, these simple soothers can quiet your chattering mind to add *oomph* to your *aaaah*.

Picture It

Combine this visualization exercise with deep-breathing techniques for a powerful stress-reducer.

1. Lie down or sit comfortably in a quiet place where you won't be disturbed. Dim the lights if you can.

2. Picture all of the negative feelings and memories of your day blobbing together into a shapeless mass of gunk. Yuck.

3. Now watch that blob start to liquify. It's melting! Watch it flow right out of your body. Feel it dripping off your fingers and toes. See it in your mind's eye, seeping into the ground and disappearing.

4. Return your thoughts to your own body. See how your mind has become clean and clear. Watch your heart, free of muck, shining brightly, bringing light to the world.

5. When you're ready, picture a stream of golden sunshine or a velvety blue glow entering your body through the crown of your head. Fill yourself up with even more light.

Take Time to Daydream

Stare out the window.

Doodle.

Indulge in a pleasant fantasy. (You're an astronaut! A pop diva!)

You're not "wasting" time — daydreaming or zoning out helps keep your brain and body on an even keel. Scientific research shows that mini mental breaks work like nutritious snacks for your brain. They help it rest and refuel.

Once refreshed, you can focus more effectively on the task at hand. You'll not only feel more contented, but you will also solve gnarly problems more easily.

Daydreaming is, quite simply, brain food.

Open a Door

Sketch a simple picture of an open door. Where will your creativity take you? Go through it to find out!

Listen to Your Heartbeat

When you're tense, or out of sorts, tuning in to the sound and feel of your inner drum can help restore your natural rhythm.

Lay your hand over your heart. Can you feel its steady beat against your palm?

Close your eyes and focus on the rhythm. Is it fast or slow? Notice if you can feel the beat elsewhere in your body, like in your fingertips or the hollow of your throat.

Consciously try to slow down your heart rate. You can do this by focusing on the sound. Using deep-breathing techniques works too.

Slowing your heart rate helps initiate the relaxation response so you feel calmer and more peaceful.

Try Progressive Relaxation

Find a quiet place where you can sit comfortably and won't be disturbed.

Close your eyes. Focus your mental attention on your left foot. Curl your toes. Tense the muscles tight, tight, tight for about five seconds. Let them go limp. Tense the muscles again — tight, tight, tight — for another five seconds, then relax. Take a few moments — about fifteen seconds — to notice how soft and heavy your foot now feels.

Continue tensing and relaxing the different muscles in your body, slowly making your way from your feet to the top of your head. When you have worked through all the muscles of your body, take a moment to savour the sensation of total relaxation.

Put Your Feet Up

Feeling down? Turn your day around by spending a few minutes in the relaxing feet-above-head position.

Stand in Tree Pose

When you feel like your life is out of whack, you can regain some balance with a yoga technique called tree pose, or vrkshasana. It will help quiet your mind as it strengthens your body.

1. Stand tall, with your feet firmly planted about hip-width apart. Rest your hands on your hips.

2. Focus your gaze on a spot straight ahead of you.

3. Slowly lift one foot off the floor, sliding the sole of your foot along the inner surface of your other leg. Let it rest comfortably above or below your knee, not on it. Press your foot into the side of your other leg.

4. If you feel like doing so, raise your arms. Hold them out to the sides, or bent at the elbows ("cactus" arms), with your hands clasped over your head or with palms pressed together in front of your heart.

5. Repeat on the other side.

Take Time to Notice

Mindfulness is the name for a number of techniques you can use to relieve stress and reduce anxiety. It trains us to notice things outside ourselves so we don't focus as much on our own everyday annoyances. It helps us live in the moment, rather than reliving the past or worrying about the future. It also helps us notice what's good in the world, allowing us to experience uplifting feelings of gratitude and joy more frequently.

Meditate

Meditation is an ancient mindfulness practice that you can do just about anywhere. Find a cozy place where you won't be disturbed. Get comfy. Close your eyes. Try not to think about anything other than the sound and feel of your own breath moving in and out of your lungs.

When a thought flits through your mind, let it go. Mentally put it on a shelf and leave it there. Keep distracting thoughts from creeping back in by focusing on a single word (like *peace*), sound (like a bell) or image (like a candle flame).

When you're ready, open your eyes and stretch.

Stay in the Moment

Even when you're out in public or pressed for time, you can still practise mindfulness.

Say silently to yourself, "I am here." Then pay careful attention to what "here" is. Observe it. Catalogue it.

What do you see, smell and hear, right at this particular, never-to-be-repeated moment?

Search for something funny or interesting or beautiful that you might not have noticed if you'd remained distracted or preoccupied. Consider that discovery a gift of love — one you've given to yourself.

Take a Mindful Walk

Hike, stroll, meander, amble. Whatever you call it, rambling on foot through the great outdoors is one of the best-known ways to reduce stress.

Add a dollop of mindfulness to your walk by paying close attention to the sights, sounds and smells around you. Do you recognize the plants and flowers? Take a closer look and really study their shapes and forms. Can you smell them? Are they attracting insects or birds? Observe them carefully — what are they doing and why? Listen to the sound of your breathing, and your footsteps on the ground.

When you walk mindfully, you see the world, and your place in it, more clearly.

Say No to Multi-tasking

Your brain is not designed to multi-task. It's designed to focus on one activity at a time. Every time you switch gears, your brain has to adapt. That takes time and energy.

Multi-tasking makes you feel like you're accomplishing more, faster, but that's an illusion. In reality, you wind up doing each task more slowly and less effectively than if you did them separately.

When you're eating lunch, watching TV, doing homework and chatting with your friend all at the same time, something is bound to fall through the cracks. You might not notice that your friend's mood has gone from buoyant to broody. Or you might overlook one of your homework questions.

So give up multi-task mayhem and opt for calm, clear focus instead.

Be Amazed

Many people find taking a walk through a curvy maze or labyrinth helps them clear their minds and relieve stress.

You don't need anything fancy to make a labyrinth. You can draw one on the sidewalk with chalk or stomp one into the snow with your feet. Make your maze so there is only one path. Arrange it so it leads into the centre of the maze and then winds its way back out.

When you emerge from the labyrinth, you may feel calmer and more centred, and have sharper focus.

Practise Clarity

The idea of meditation is simple, but it takes practice. It's very common to find your thoughts wandering off when you're "supposed" to be keeping it clear. Don't worry if they do — the more you practise, the easier it will get.

Enjoy the Sound of Silence

People of all faiths have gone on silent retreats since time immemorial. That's because simply being quiet can be soothing to the mind, soul and body.

Find a place where you can tune everything out — the school library or your bathtub. Put on headphones or block out noise with ear plugs.

As the noises of the world disappear, so might your troubles. You might even be able to hear the whisperings of your own heart.

Let the sound of silence quiet your mind and free your soul.

A Matter of Deep Gravity

Gravity is one of the main forces at work in the universe. It controls how objects of different mass and size behave in relation to one another. Thanks to gravity, larger objects, like the sun, draw smaller ones, like planets, toward them. Gravity is the universe's way of giving heavenly bodies a hug.

Here on Earth, gravity is also giving you a celestial embrace. To feel it, lie on your back flat on the floor. Give yourself a few moments to feel, deeply, how the ground supports you. The Earth itself is holding you tight to her heart.

Earth literally keeps you grounded and supported.

Move Your Body

Your body was built to move. Whether you walk, run, dance, swim, skate or rock climb, you're doing exactly what your body is designed to do.

But what does that have to do with your stress-management plan? A LOT.

Adrenalin, one of the hormone that is triggered by stress, prepares your body for fight-or-flight. It speeds up your heart rate and oxygen intake and sends more power to your muscles.

While adrenalin levels remain high, you may feel tense and anxious. Going for a run or doing push-ups will help relieve those feelings by redirecting the adrenalin into exercise.

As you exercise, the drop in adrenalin levels triggers the relaxation response (page 30), which generates feelings of contentment and relaxation.

So the more you move, the calmer and happier you'll feel — even when you're not climbing mountains.

Put a Bounce in Your Step

If you've taken any mindful walks (page 47) lately, you might have noticed how you walk. Do you slouch or drag your heels, bow your shoulders or gaze at your feet or phone? Or do you hold your head high, with your shoulders back and your chest open?

Maintaining good posture while standing and walking can really lift your mood. Relaxing your shoulders and lifting your chin sends the message to your brain that you are relaxed and confident. Opening your chest makes more room inside your rib cage for your lungs. That lets them take in more oxygen, and that, in turn, makes you feel more energized.

A determined, strong stride will also strengthen your muscles and boost your aerobic fitness.

Best of all, it feels good.

The Home Stretch

Stretching helps you loosen up. It increases blood flow to your muscles and encourages tight muscle fibres to loosen, helping the rest of you relax too.

A stretching session also gives you the perfect opportunity to practise mindfulness. As you do each stretch, focus on the sensations in your body. Can you feel the muscle fibres release? How does a particular stretch feel on the left side of your body compared to the right?

When you stretch, keep it gentle. Stretching should feel good, not painful. Hold each stretch for thirty to sixty seconds (or longer if it feels right for you). Keep your focus on your breathing throughout the stretch.

Start off easy by raising your hands over your head as high as you can. Stretch even higher. Lift onto your tippytoes to take you even higher.

After each stretch, do a counter-stretch — a gentle twist or turn in the opposite direction. That helps keep muscles from seizing up or going into spasm.

Let It All Out

Your perspiration contains all the hormones circulating throughout your body, including the stress hormones adrenalin and cortisol. As your sweat leaves your body, so do the stress hormones. Your feelings of distress literally evaporate!

Make It Aerobic

Aerobic exercise gets you out of breath and sweaty. It gets your heart pumping harder too. It's fun, and it's good for you. By redirecting adrenalin into exercise, you are transforming the way you respond to it, which helps you get to a more relaxed state.

So go ahead — get moving. You don't need a lot of time, a team sport or a fancy gym to do it. At home, at the park, on your way home from school — there are plenty of opportunities to get moving.

Run up and down a flight of stairs before lunch or take a ten-minute break from your homework by cranking some tunes and dancing around the kitchen. Even carrying in the groceries can do the trick by raising your heart rate.

Getting hot and sweaty at least twenty to thirty minutes a day is a super way to keep your cool all day long.

Mix It Up

There are thousands of different forms of physical activity out there. Some build strength, others build endurance, flexibility or coordination. All of them contribute to mental and emotional well-being. By choosing from a variety of activities, you keep your mind engaged and your whole body healthy.

Finding activities you enjoy matters a lot. If you don't have fun while you're doing something, it's unlikely you'll stick with it. Mixing it up matters too. Even if you adore badminton, you might get bored if it's the only activity you do. Engaging in a range of physical activities helps keep it fresh and also gives you the greatest whole-body benefits.

Physical activity doesn't always mean sports or games. Hiking, dancing, even twirling around in circles or mastering bouncing on a pogo stick fits the bill.

Fuel Your Body

Stress can be described as a physical process that arises when you find yourself in a challenging situation. It can also happen at the microscopic level, inside the cells of your body, when the cells themselves are challenged. And stressed-out cells contribute to a stressed-out you.

Your cells act like tiny furnaces. They need fuel in order to keep working, performing essential tasks like building new muscle tissue, pumping blood and fighting infections. Since we can't get energy from sunlight like green plants do, human beings and all other animals have to get energy from food.

When you eat the kinds of foods your cells need, you'll have more energy and stamina. You'll feel calmer and less irritable. And you'll have more resilience so you can bounce back from stressful situations.

Eat a Good Breakfast

You might have heard people say that breakfast is the most important meal of the day. That's because you can't eat while you snooze. When you wake up in the morning, it's like you've been fasting all night long. And without food in your stomach, your personal fuel tank is on *E* for *Empty*.

Breakfast — breaking the fast — is the way to refill your tank so you can have the energy to get through your day.

The best breakfasts are ones that include complex carbohydrates, like bran muffins or oatmeal, proteins like tofu or eggs, healthy fats like yogurt, nuts or olives, and a variety of fruits or vegetables. They'll keep you on an even keel all morning long.

Charge Up!

After a night's fasting, a good breakfast will replenish the blood sugar levels that your body needs to charge up your brain and muscles for a busy day.

Don't Skip Meals

An empty tummy is a grumbly tummy! It's also a signal that it's time to eat and refuel again.

If you ignore that signal and skip a meal, you force your body to work harder to do everyday tasks. It winds up burning the extra fuel your body stores for emergencies or for tough workouts. You'll feel tired faster and be more likely to catch colds. You might also feel more irritable and less able to concentrate.

Eating regular meals ensures you'll have the *oomph* you need to deal with whatever life throws at you.

Snack Attack!

Eating several times throughout the day is a good strategy for keeping your fuel tank full and your stress level low. Avoid overeating by choosing healthy foods and taking smaller portions.

How Not to Get Hangry

When your body's low on fuel and working extra hard to keep going, you might get "hangry" — that mixture of hungry and angry that makes it difficult to concentrate and get along with other people.

To avoid getting hangry, make sure your snacks and meals contain a combination of foods that will keep you feeling satisfied for longer.

In general, carbohydrates tend to zip through your digestive system, while proteins linger longer. Fats take the most time to digest.

You'll feel hungry faster if you eat a meal made up mostly of carbs or sweets. If you add in fats and proteins, you'll stay satiated longer.

H-A-L-T

Before you fly off the handle, HALT and ask yourself:

Are you **H**ungry? If so, go eat something.

Are you **A**ngry? If so, give yourself a time out to calm down and sort through your feelings.

Are you **L**onely? Seek out some companionship and support.

Are you **T**ired? Take a break or a nap, or hit the hay for the night.

Avoid the Junk Food Trap

Back in prehistory, people had to work hard hunting animals and gathering fruit, nuts and seeds to obtain vital nutrients: protein, fat and sugar. They might not have gone to the trouble if those foods didn't taste great!

Nowadays, most of us have easy access to sweet or greasy foods. You know eating too many junk foods like chips, sugary pop and cookies, however, can harm your health and leave you vulnerable to stress. But your taste buds don't know that! They still work exactly like our prehistoric ancestors' did.

Your modern mind, therefore, needs to watch out for junk-food traps. Make a conscious decision to limit the amount of sweet or fatty foods you eat because you know the harm they can cause.

Are You Thirsty?

Sometimes people confuse thirst signals for hunger. Drink some water before you reach for a snack.

Drink More Water

Did you know your body is essentially a bag of sea water? Long, long ago, our ancestors were ocean animals. Our cells evolved to live in salty water.

When they left the ocean, our ancestors took some of that water with them — inside their bodies. Even now, we still need that water for our cells to work. And when we don't have enough of it flowing through our bodies, we are more vulnerable to stress, both physically and emotionally.

To make sure we stay hydrated, our bodies have a way to warn us when our water levels are low. It's called thirst. If you drink water when you feel thirsty, you will be less likely to get dehydrated.

Rest Your Body

Do you love curling up under the covers? Do you really enjoy a day spent lazing around in your PJs?

No, you're not a lazy bones if you savour sack time. When you sleep, your body is actually working hard. It's repairing damage to cells, saving memories and restoring supplies of essential elements.

Sleep is essential to your health. Getting a good night's sleep, every night, is protection against negative stress too.

Catch Some ZZZZs

If you often find you're dragging your keister just to get through the day, you might not be getting enough sleep.

Most kids need at least eight hours of sleep each night. Because your body is still growing, you may need a lot more.

To find out how much more, keep a sleep journal. Record what time you went to bed and what time you woke up for the course of one week. Jot down how you felt every morning.

At the end of the week, add up the total number of hours and divide by seven to get your nightly average.

If you frequently felt tired in the morning, your nightly average is probably too low for you. Try getting into bed earlier for a few days and see if you feel more energetic. If so, you know you'll have to make time for more sack time.

Pay Back Your Sleep Debt

You've discovered that you really need nine to ten hours of sleep each night to feel your best. But your schedule is so busy (morning hockey practice, after-school art club, late-night homework), you regularly clock less than eight. If this description sounds like you, you can wind up with what experts call a sleep debt or sleep deficit.

Sleep debt can make you feel sleepy. But not everyone with sleep debt does. People can get used to it. They stop noticing they don't feel their best.

But chronic sleep debt affects your ability to think. It weakens your immune system and contributes to conditions like heart disease and diabetes.

So how do you pay back your sleep debt? Prepare to put in lots of extra snooze time. According to sleep experts, it can take up to four days to make up for one hour of lost sleep, and nine to completely recover from a significant sleep deficit.

Are You Sleepy?

Three signs you're not getting enough sleep:

- You find it difficult to get up in the morning.
- You have trouble focusing.
- You are drowsy, and sometimes even nod off, during the day.

Take a Nap

Setting up a regular sleep schedule (getting up at around the same time every morning, even on weekends) and sticking to it is a proven way to ensure you get the rest you need.

But that doesn't mean you should skip accepting your Oscar so you can get your beauty sleep. If you get less sleep than usual for a night or two, it won't cause you any real problem. Taking a nap can get you back on track.

The ideal nap is short — less than 45 minutes. And you should wake feeling alert or energized, not groggier than when you conked out.

Take one when you feel out of gas — it will refill your energy tank — or to turbocharge your batteries before a physically or mentally demanding event, like the big track meet or chemistry mid-term.

Get Set to Sleep

You're in your jammies, ready to hit the hay. These tips can help you drop off to dreamland faster, and stay sound asleep until the birds start twittering, "Good morning!"

- Dim the lights half an hour before you turn in. That sends an "it's sleepy time!" signal to your brain.
- Avoid screens right before bed. The blue light interferes with quality sleep.
- Take a warm bath or shower before bed. When you get out of the warm water, your body naturally starts to cool down — and that triggers the hormones that make you feel sleepy.
- Avoid caffeine at least six hours before bed.
- Exercise four to six hours before bed.
- Do your homework after exercise when your mind is calmest, clearest and most focused. Then give yourself some R & R time between homework and bedtime.
- Use your bed only for sleeping. No homework, no texting!

Switch Up Your Routine

If you have trouble falling asleep, changing up your routine can sometimes help break the cycle. Get out of bed and do something dull, like brushing your teeth. Read a boring bit of a book (on paper, not a screen), like the index of this book. Do a short, soothing yoga practice or try a progressive relaxation technique. Return to bed when you feel sleepy.

Write Down Your Worries

When you try to turn in, do unwanted worries keep you from settling in and dropping off to snoozeland? To defeat the worry monster and get the sleep you need, jot down a brief description of what's worrying you. Now set it aside. Tell yourself you'll deal with it in the morning. In doing so, you give yourself permission to get to sleep.

Jam the Circuits

You can stop your brain from rehashing troubling thoughts by intentionally jamming the circuits.

Simply give your brain something else to think about. Choose something mildly challenging but utterly dull. For example, you can make a mental list of all vegetables you've eaten — or refused to eat.

While your mind is busy making a list of lettuces (romaine AND iceberg), it can't focus on the more troubling thoughts that keep you awake. You'll sleep like a baby spinach.

Turn a New Page

As you prepare for bed, take a few moments to mentally review your day. Paste the events of that day into an imaginary scrapbook. Turn the page when you turn out the lights.

In the morning, you'll wake up to a bright, clean page.

Start Fresh

A fresh start.

A clean slate.

A shiny new day.

What will you create from it?

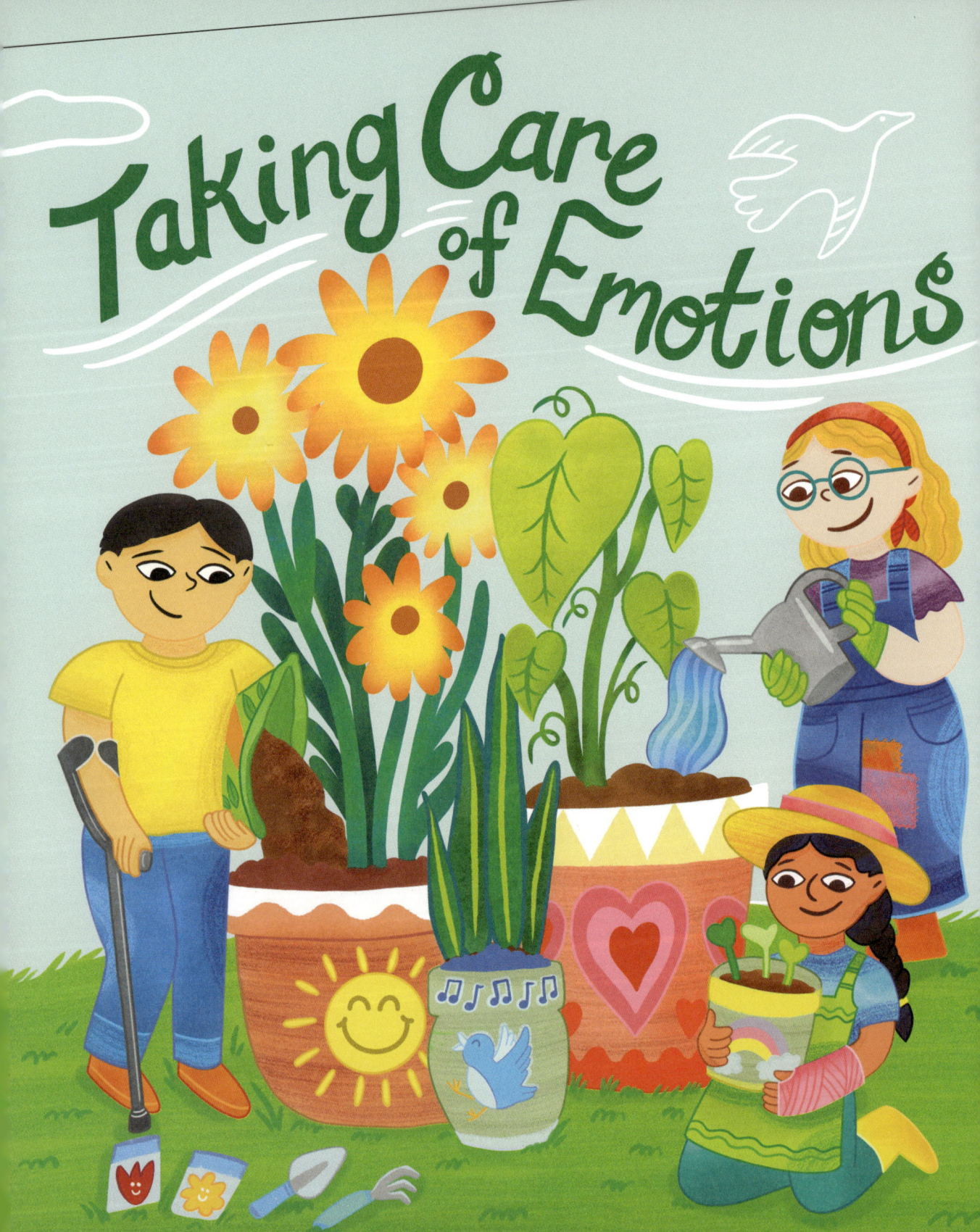

PART 3

Your feelings matter. Acknowledging them, expressing them and reacting appropriately to them also matters.

As you become more attuned to your emotions, you get better at handling life's stressors. And when you share how you feel with other people — and listen when they share their feelings with you — you deepen personal relationships. You gradually build a network of supportive friends and family, one of the best stress relievers out there. Experts in stress management say people with positive social networks cope better with stress than others.

In this section you'll find suggestions for how to become more aware and responsive to your emotions. You'll also learn ways to build better relationships with the people in your life so you can create your own stress-smashing social network. You will explore your creative side to express your feelings, and learn helpful self-care practices for keeping your emotions from spinning out of control.

Connect with Your Emotions

You can improve your ability to identify your feelings by sorting them into basic categories. One well-known grouping suggests these six: happiness, sadness, fear, disgust, anger, surprise.

Once you've figured out which category your sensations fall into, look at how intense the emotions feel. Feeling happy? How happy? Mildly, moderately or over-the-moon intensely?

Then consider what else you might be feeling at the same time. If you are joyful (very happy) but also nervous (mild fear), the overall emotion you feel might be called something like excitement or anticipation.

Listen to Your Gut

Your mind works quickly. Even so, the chemical and electrical messages it sends can sometimes arrive in your gut faster than they reach the decision-making part of your brain. You might feel these signals as a twist in your belly or a flutter of joy in your heart, without immediately knowing why.

Some people call these feelings intuition. Others call them having a hunch or a gut feeling. No matter what you call them, listen to them. They know things about you and your surroundings that you may not know yourself.

Listen to Your Second Brain!

Did you know you actually have a second "brain" inside your belly? The lining of your digestive system contains more than 100 million neurons, the kind of cells that make up nerves and brain tissue.

Let It Out

Do you ever stifle your feelings and keep them bottled up inside? That's a common reaction to negative feelings.

There are times when it makes sense to keep our feelings to ourselves, like when you are with people you don't trust or when you need to cool down before saying something you'll regret. But if you do that all the time, you might cause more harm than good.

Holding in and holding on to distressing emotions like fear, anger or sadness can sometimes make them worse. It can make you more prone to emotional outbursts — when the emotions pour out of you in uncontrolled and damaging ways. It can even make you physically sick.

Instead of holding them in, find effective ways to share your feelings.

Express Yourself

Instead of ignoring or suppressing your feelings, let them out in a safe way. First, allow yourself to acknowledge the feeling. For example, you may have told your cousin "That's okay" when he broke your unicorn figurine. And you meant it — you knew it was an accident. But it's also okay to acknowledge to yourself that you feel hurt, sad and angry.

Once you accept your feelings as real, find an outlet where you can express them safely. Write down how you really feel in a private journal. Or tell a caring friend about what happened and how it affected you. Some people share their feelings with the trees.

Expressing negative emotions can be difficult, but it also feels good. You might also come up with ways to solve problems as you talk about them.

So Many Feelings!

According to some psychologists, there are eight basic emotions. Other psychologists say there are nine or twelve. Charles Darwin thought there were thirty-four. Some researchers believe there are as many as 34,000 discrete emotions! No wonder you sometimes have trouble sorting out your feelings.

Reserve Judgment

Feelings aren't good or bad. They are simply messengers that communicate to your brain how different experiences affect you. Frustration, pride, joy — every feeling is valid.

Some people believe that having certain feelings, like anger, makes them a bad person. Not true. *Everyone* gets angry now and then. What matters is what you do in response to those feelings.

All the Feels!

Your feelings are your own. You are entitled to them. And you deserve for them to be respected.

Visit Your Happy Place

When you're feeling down, distressed or upset, try this visualization technique to improve your mood.

Think about a place you really love, or one where you are safe and loved. Picture it in your mind in as much detail as possible.

Whenever you vividly imagine your happy place, your brain generates the same feelings you'd have if you were really there. You might feel your muscles relax and your breathing slow and deepen. Stress melts away.

Visiting your happy place regularly can be a super tool for keeping your mind and body calm and contented.

Jump for Joy

Delight.

Pride.

Awe.

Gratitude.

Misery might love company, but joy adores a party.

Savour your positive feelings. Express them, share them, spread them around.

Keep a Gratitude Journal

A gratitude journal helps you stay focused on the positive. Make it a daily habit to jot down something that happened during your day for which you are grateful. If you've had a tough day, this can be daunting. But finding reasons for gratitude gets easier with practice.

Be Kind to Yourself

You've dropped your mittens in the mud. *Argh!* Don't spend the rest of your day beating yourself up. Acknowledge that everybody makes mistakes. Accidents happen. Move on.

Take Regular Mental Health Breaks

You already know that sleep is important for repairing and replenishing your brain and body. But so is taking a break. Taking five to stretch your legs partway through a study session isn't procrastination; it's a smart way to refresh yourself. Changing things up improves your ability to concentrate and helps prevent fatigue and frustration. Taking regular mental health breaks will also help you maintain your emotional equilibrium, keeping you calm and centred throughout the day.

Make Personal Connections

The relationships you have with others are the heart of being human. Our species is social — like ants, lions or dogs — meaning we have evolved to function best as part of a group. And we feel happiest and safest when we feel a sense of belonging and connection to others.

So feeling isolated, shut out or lonely is a very real source of stress. It feels terrible and, over an extended period of time, can harm your health.

Being able to create and maintain strong bonds with others, therefore, is an important part of any stress-management practice. In this section, you'll find suggestions for building and maintaining a strong social network.

Share Your Feelings

Sharing your feelings with others is a great way to relieve stress. It's also a time-honoured way to build and strengthen relationships.

When you share your true feelings with a friend or relative, you might find out that they feel the same way or have had similar experiences. Both of you also gain a deeper understanding about each other's likes and dislikes. That helps build enduring bonds between you.

Strong social connections can help you survive stormy seas. And having that close ally to share successes and joy with doubles the delight when you arrive safely in harbour.

Say It in Person

The best way to share your feelings is by talking them over in person.

Make More Eye Contact

Talking with your teacher? Approaching the new kid? It's tempting to avoid making direct eye contact, especially if you're struggling to come up with the right thing to say.

But making eye contact is an important way to build connections with others. It triggers the release of oxytocin, a hormone that makes people feel affectionate for one another.

People's eyes tell you a lot about them. Enlarged pupils can signal they're interested, excited, scared or concentrating intensely. Movements in the muscles around their eyes can communicate emotions too.

WHEN TO LOOK AWAY

Making eye contact is so powerful, there are times when it is smart to look away. That direct gaze can make you feel very self-conscious and it can be so distracting that your ability to concentrate, remember and solve problems is temporarily weakened.

Synchronize Your Brain with Someone Else's

You know that feeling you get when you are totally in sync with someone else? When you know what they're thinking, even before they do? That's not an illusion. During a meeting of the minds, your brain activity and the other person's become more similar.

As your brains sync up, so does your behaviour. You and your partner might wind up using similar gestures or speech patterns, unconsciously imitating each other.

This incredible phenomenon is called brain-to-brain synchrony, and it's a genius-level stress beater. It enhances feelings of closeness and belonging. It builds trust, empathy and a sense of community, all of which contribute to more numerous and deeper social relationships.

So how can you create more magic moments of brain-to-brain synchrony?

Looking someone in the eye works. Collaborating on a project also builds mental synchronization, as does discussing a new and exciting idea or participating in a team sport.

Team Up

If you've ever played a team sport, you know how much fun it can be. But team sports also help you manage stress. When you're part of a team, you're a member of a community. Those social connections keep you emotionally resilient.

As your teammates work together to achieve a goal, you get more chances to achieve feel-good brain-to-brain synchrony. And all that sweaty exercise helps you blow off steam — literally.

You don't need to consider yourself an athlete to join a team. Intramural and community-centre leagues offer recreational options for kids who just want to have fun.

Be a Team Player

Be a team player — both on and off the field. Be generous with your time. Share your knowledge. Lend a hand to others.

When you're there for others, they'll be there for you when you need them. Isn't that a comforting thought?

Ace of Clubs

The teams you join don't need to be sports-related. You can play oboe in the school band, sculpt clay at the after-school art club or compete in the robotics league. Whatever your interests, you can find like-minded folks to pursue them with.

Whether you're making 3-D printed figurines or learning how to bake a lemon meringue pie, you'll make new friends, get a break from your daily routine and enjoy the incomparable feeling of being part of a community.

The Art of Giving

Is it really better to give than to receive? It's hard to believe that old saying is true. How could having less be better than having more?

First of all, when you get rid of clutter, you create a less stressful environment for yourself. You no longer have to clean or store things. You gain time and space for yourself.

Even more importantly, giving away unwanted possessions generates oodles of feel-good vibes, because helping others is one of the strongest boosters of self-esteem out there. It feels great to know you can contribute to your community in a meaningful way.

But giving doesn't apply only to things. Generosity of spirit — when you give your time, your attention or your understanding — might be the most rewarding form of giving. Freely giving away a piece of yourself doesn't diminish you. It enhances you.

Give More than You Get

It's a fact. When you give of yourself — by sharing your smiles and hugs, by offering support or assistance or by doing something nice for someone else — you will absolutely, positively, 110 percent get back more in return.

Giving feels good in a variety of ways:

- It gives you pleasure to know that your gift might make a real difference to another person.
- You develop friendships and build trust and loyalty.
- It feels good to be appreciated when someone says "thank you."
- You can feel proud that you are a generous and thoughtful person.

These are all gifts worth giving — to yourself.

Pay It Forward

Your classmate did you a favour by sharing notes from the day you were sick. Of course you should pay them back when you can by doing something kind for them. But you can also pay it forward, by doing something kind for someone else.

The idea of paying it forward became popular after a book and a movie called *Pay It Forward*. The story suggests that when someone does a good turn for you, you can multiply the positivity in the world by paying it forward — doing a good turn for three other people. In all corners of the globe, people started engaging in random acts of kindness, paying good deeds forward, sometimes even anonymously. Why? Because it felt great!

Get Personal

Paying it forward personally yields longer-lasting stress relief than random, anonymous acts.

Become a Mentor

Take a moment to appreciate all the skills you've developed since you were little. You had plenty of help from parents, caregivers, teachers and mentors.

A mentor is someone who takes an interest in you, who encourages you, who helps you reach your goals. Anyone can be a mentor — an older sister, a neighbour, an aunt or a piano teacher. Even you!

Becoming a mentor to someone else is another way of paying it forward. It's a very powerful one, because you can really change a person's life.

Practise Self-Care!

Between school work and chores, you have tons of responsibilities. When you've checked off the tasks on your to-do list, is there any time left for YOU?

Carving out me time and spending those precious moments exactly how you want to is as important as the other chores on your list. And there are lots of reasons why:

- You are the star of your own life. Your hopes and dreams deserve attention.
- Joy is essential. Just like water and nutritious food, you need plenty of joy to keep yourself healthy.
- You can't do all the things you want or need to do if you're burnt-out or exhausted.

The suggestions in this section will help you create me time and use it wisely to strengthen your spirit and body.

Learn from the Garden

Whether they're growing crops for food or cultivating a pretty windowsill geranium, gardeners know that plants don't thrive unless they have the right conditions. Green plants need lots of sunlight and plenty of water. And since growing takes time, they also need heaps of patience.

You also need sunshine and fresh air. You need plenty of water. And because growing takes time, you should also treat yourself with patient kindness.

Take care of yourself and you'll bloom.

The Self-Care Triangle

Practise self-care by taking care of your body, your mind and your heart.

Stick to a Routine

Keeping a predictable daily routine is one way to make sure you get enough me time. Here's how to make one work for you.

1. Draw a calendar showing a single week. Divide each day into hourly segments.

2. Block off the time you're in school each day, plus the time getting there and back.

3. Mark off any regular before- or after-school activities.

4. Decide what time you have to get up in the morning to get to school on time without rushing. Mark it on your calendar for every day of the week, even weekends.

5. Mark your bedtime on your calendar for every day of the week. Keep in mind how much sleep you need to feel your best (page 65).

6. On a separate piece of paper, list all the activities that fill your day. Slot them into your calendar.

7. Make a separate list of all the self-care activities you would like to include regularly in your routine. These can include meditation, reading, hanging out with friends, watching movies or sports, drawing . . . Add these to your calendar.

If you're like most people, there won't be a lot of time in your schedule for all of your self-care activities. Do your best to sprinkle them around, making sure there are at least a few of them every day. Remember: five minutes of quiet reflection is better than zero.

Tweak Your Routine

Now that you have a basic plan, stick to it! It won't be easy at first. You may have underestimated how long each activity takes or forgotten to account for some. That's okay — revise your schedule as necessary.

Follow your routine as closely as you can for a week. At the end of the week, review it.

How well did you stick to it? And more importantly, how do you feel? Do you feel more energetic or less stressed? If so, that will make it easier to stick to your feel-good plan next week.

Make adjustments to your routine so it works even better, and try it again next week. Before you know it, feeling calm, well rested and capable will become, well, routine!

Be Flexible

Give yourself permission to be flexible, to change it up as you see fit. Stay up as late as you want at that sleepover! Simply return to your regular schedule the next day, but with the addition of some extra recovery time.

Reward Yourself

One way to keep yourself feeling top-notch is by rewarding yourself in your own way, whenever you think you deserve it.

The rewards you give yourself can be simple, even silly. Looking at yourself in the mirror and saying, "You are AMAZING!" might be one. So can allowing yourself five minutes to play a game or doodling kooky portraits of alien elephants. Indulge yourself in a little luxury, like a long soak in a fragrant bubble bath. Or give yourself a soothing self-massage — it's a literal pat on the back!

Learn from the Wall

Ever feel like you've – *boomf!* – hit the wall? That wall is there for a reason. It's telling you to lean up against it and rest. It's telling you to take a break. Listen to it.

A Handy Reward

This reward is literally right at your fingertips!

Give your hard-working hands a well-earned treat with this stress-relieving finger massage.

1. Choose a moisturizer with a pleasant scent.

2. Starting with one of your pinkies, gently rub each finger.

3. Massage your palms. Pay special attention to the pad by your thumb.

4. Stretch your fingers wide, then relax them.

5. Make tight fists, then relax them.

6. Rotate your wrists in both directions.

Ahhh . . .

Practise Positive Self-Talk

You already know the value of speaking kindly to other people. Speaking kindly to and about yourself also brings major plusses.

Positive self-talk keeps you from exaggerating negative feelings. When you give yourself a private pep talk, it helps you stay motivated and on task. You'll also become more resilient when you're stressed and be better at managing criticism from others.

To practise positive self-talk, pay attention to the thoughts running through your head. Do you regularly call yourself names ("I'm such a loser") or run yourself down ("Nobody likes me")?

When you notice this happening — STOP. Replace that negative thought with more positive ones. ("No, I'm not a loser; I just made a mistake, and I'll do better next time.")

When you use positive language on yourself, you feel better about yourself. You become more likely to reach your goals. And when you treat yourself kindly, other people will do so as well.

Mind Your Words

Pay attention to the words you use about yourself, both in your head and out loud. Are you using words that highlight your strengths? Or do you tend to use negative words that underscore your weaknesses?

Talk Yourself through It

Most positive self-talk takes place inside your own mind. Another kind of positive self-talk is done out loud. It helps you achieve difficult tasks.

By talking yourself through a challenge, you become your own coach and fan club. Imagine, for example, you're making a chocolate layer cake for your sister's birthday. There are a lot of steps, and you're nervous about missing one.

Talk yourself through the steps as you collect your ingredients. Read them off your list out loud.

When your ingredients are assembled on the counter, ask yourself aloud, "What am I missing?" Your ear might pick up something your eyes don't.

Continue coaching yourself through each step. If something goes wrong, ask yourself what a good coach would say. They might cheer, "You got this!" They might tell you, "You can figure out how to make this work." Or if they think you need it, they might call for a time out.

Say those same encouraging words to yourself. Take that cake break and come back to the task renewed. Your cake will be wonderful (even if the icing is lopsided)!

The Myth of Perfection

News flash: You're not perfect. No one is. That's a good thing.

Once you stop reaching for the impossible, you find something even better: a world of endless opportunity. You'll be:

- free of false expectations
- free to fail
- free to be yourself

The Beauty of Imperfection

Around the world, art objects are intentionally made with at least one imperfection in them. The flaw is meant to reflect the belief that nothing in life can ever be perfect, and beauty comes from the imperfection.

The Navajo people of the Southwest United States, for example, intentionally weave small irregularities called spirit lines into their stunning geometric rugs.

Similarly, Islamic art and architecture is often created with an intentional flaw — a missing line or less-than-perfect symmetry. The reason? That only Allah can achieve true perfection.

Meanwhile, in Japan, artists have been celebrating imperfection since as early as the sixteenth century. An aesthetic idea called wabi-sabi promotes asymmetry, roughness and even cracks and other signs of wear as hallmarks of true beauty.

And in Dutch art of the Golden Age (the seventeenth century), still-life paintings frequently depict sumptuous arrangements of fruit or flowers. Despite their splendour, the scenes usually include fly-in-the-ointment details: creepy insects, wilting blooms or rotting fruit. The idea is to remind viewers that nothing is perfect and that everything changes. What appears perfect today will be gone tomorrow.

Channel Your Creative Side

Creativity is part of what makes us human. It can come in infinite forms: making music, programming an app, building an awesome snow fort or designing an inspirational collage. You don't even have to be "good" at it — whenever you let your imagination go, you are honouring a fundamental part of your being.

Creative expression is also a key component of self-care. When you engage in creative work or play, you get to express yourself, to share your feelings and perspectives with others. And that feels good.

But you also get to experience more moments of flow — a stress-relieving sensation that leads to deeper and long-lasting feelings of joy and contentment.

The suggestions in this section will help stimulate your creative juices and get your imagination going.

Fill Your Well

Many artists think of their creativity like water flowing from a well or spring. As long as the water source remains constant, the creativity flows. But if the well goes empty or the spring dries up, so does their imagination.

An important aspect of creativity, then, is keeping your well full. You do that by pouring in lots of the good stuff — stimulating experiences, healthy food, meditation and time with friends and family.

Go with the Flow

When you're completely immersed in an activity you enjoy, you might find yourself in a unique psychological state called flow. In flow (sometimes called the zone), time vanishes. So does the outside world. You are so completely focused on what you're doing, you might not notice that your belly is rumbling or that people are speaking to you. You perform tasks in flow without conscious thought, almost automatically.

Flow feels great when you're in it. It also brings plenty of other stress-relieving benefits:

- It increases your ability to control your emotions.
- It increases your feelings of motivation and engagement.
- It helps you build perseverance and develop new skills.
- It improves your ability to learn, concentrate and focus.
- It builds self-confidence.
- It encourages feelings of well-being and empathy.

Everyone can experience flow, but you will be more likely to do so if you are engaging in an activity that you're doing simply for your own pleasure or satisfaction, rather than an external reward.

Don't Flow It Alone

At least not all the time. People report their most meaningful experiences of flow happen when they are in a group, working and talking with each other.

How to Get Flow Going

To enjoy all the benefits of flow, you have to give it the opportunity to happen. These suggestions will help you find the zone:

- Choose an activity you love. The more fun you are having, the easier it will be to achieve flow.

- Setting realistic limits, like "I'm going to write and draw page one of my graphic novel" is preferable to grand, unfocused dreams like, "I'm going to write a book." You'll be more likely to achieve a flow state if you have a clear, achievable short-term goal.

- Get rid of distractions. Reaching flow takes time and concentration, so guarding yourself from interruptions and competing attention grabbers is essential.

- Make it tough, but not too tough. Very easy activities won't hold your attention. Tasks that are too hard will leave you frustrated. Flow comes easiest when your skill level and the task difficulty level are matched. You'll have to stretch yourself to succeed, but if you stick with it, you know you'll be able to achieve your goal.

- Self-criticism will keep you locked out of the zone. Give yourself permission to follow your instincts. And remind yourself that there's no right way or wrong way to learn, grow or create.

Make Space for Creativity

Some environments stimulate creativity. Others squash it.

For many people, a serene atmosphere works best. Soft hues and uncluttered countertops act like a blank canvas for your ideas. The colours blue and green help some people feel more productive. Others enjoy the playfulness that comes from a mixture of colours. Either way, keep your creative space a calm oasis. That will also lower your stress level.

Get Inspired

The Latin root of the word *inspiration* means "to breathe into." This suggests that flow (artistic inspiration) can be stimulated by deep, restorative breathing.

Take a Shower

When you take a shower, the sound of the water is about 70 decibels – as loud as a coffee shop!

So if you're short of ideas, take a short stint under the nozzle for a cascade of new ideas.

Fine-Tune the Volume

For many people, noise is a terrible source of stress. At high levels, or if it comes unpredictably, it can be downright painful.

So you might think the most soothing environment — and the one best for creative pursuits — is one that is completely silent.

Think again.

Research shows that a moderately noisy environment — about as noisy as a busy classroom — is best for stimulating new ideas.

Need ways to bring your creative space to the optimum noise level? Leave your bedroom door open so you can hear the everyday sounds your family and pets make. Play some music. Or tune in to an audio file of waves breaking on a beach, birds twittering or even a virtual coffee shop!

Hum a Tune

You can make your own just-the-right-level soundtrack by humming while you work. Not only will the sound help you focus, but humming will make you feel calmer and happier too!

When you hum, your whole body vibrates slightly. That's like a mini internal massage. It can also stimulate the relaxation response, making you feel more peaceful and contented.

Make Beautiful Music

It doesn't matter if you're tone-deaf — everyone can make beautiful music. Sing along with your favourite song or bang out a funky rhythm on the bottom of a pot — you'll be making your own unique creative contribution to the cosmic concert.

You don't need to be "good" at it — life isn't always about performing in front of an audience. It's enough to please an audience of one — you.

Music helps your body find its inner rhythm. Let it move your soul.

The Joy of Music!

Singing or playing an instrument triggers the release of neurotransmitters called endorphins, which make you feel joyful. In fact, making music of all kinds builds brain power and health. It's also a great way to find and increase rewarding moments of flow.

Write in a Journal

Keeping a diary or journal is a great way to create a record of your memories. It's also a wonderful way to help you create. Period.

There are no rules for what you put in your journal. You can write a funny poem about your feet or a horror story about your disastrous day. You can use coloured pencils to capture the riot of activity in the schoolyard, or markers to sketch out your idea for an awesome treehouse.

What you include in your journal is completely up to you. You can turn it into a work of art or a personal tool for sorting out your feelings.

You can experiment and explore with words, pictures, ideas . . . And that's the essence of creativity!

Keep a Pocket Journal

Out for a stroll or hanging out in the park? Whenever you leave your home, take along your journal.

Record random thoughts as they occur, no matter how odd. Draw a quick pic of something you see: a dramatic sunset, an oddly angled branch that looks like a toothbrush.

Your pocket notebook will help keep you mindful while you're out and about. You'll never be bored!

And when you're back at home, you can use it for inspiration.

Draw

Do you consider yourself "good" at drawing?

While being able to accurately draw objects involves some basic talent, it's actually a skill that anyone can learn. Whether or not you become the next Rembrandt, it's one worth developing.

When you try to capture what you see around you, it forces you to focus intensely. That helps you get into the zone. The repetitive motion of your hand and eyes soothes the nervous system and helps trigger the relaxation response.

Drawing sharpens your observation skills too. You'll be amazed how much more you notice — the intricate web of a garden spider or the shifting shadows on the sidewalk — after even a brief sketch session.

Don't worry if you aren't "good" at it. Drawing is about expressing yourself, not about rendering a photographic representation of an object (a camera can do that!). Besides, you get benefits from the act of drawing, not just what you wind up with on the page. And if you practise, you will naturally get better at controlling your hand.

Drawing will help you see the world in a new way — literally.

How to Improve Your Drawing and Observation Skills

1. Focus on basic shapes. If you are drawing a dog, mentally divide the body into its components – a rectangle for the body, a circle or triangle for the head, etc. Sketch these lightly on your paper.

2. Draw in the boundaries around each shape.

3. If you are having trouble seeing the boundaries clearly, close one eye as you look at your subject. That will make the three-dimensional shape look more two-dimensional – flatter – and might make it easier to draw.

4. Look at the white, or negative, space around your subject. Sometimes you will have an easier time finding boundaries and shapes by focusing on the shapes around it.

5. Turn the page upside down. By turning your subject upside down, it helps you stop seeing the dog statue you're drawing as a dog and instead as meaningless shapes.

6. Add depth by lightly sketching in shadows. Pay attention to the light and dark spots on and around your subject. Use the side of your pencil and an eraser to emphasize them.

7. Practise. The more daily practice you do, the better you will become at being able to capture your ideas on paper.

PART 4

From this book so far, you've learned a wide variety of tactics to help you become more resilient and less vulnerable to the negative effects of stress. But stress is a part of life. You can't avoid it totally.

When you find yourself in the hot seat, you'll need effective strategies to use in the moment. With the tips in this section, you'll be able to reduce the grip of the stress response on your mind and body. You'll learn ways to react more positively in a crisis and to make better decisions.

When You're Feeling Overwhelmed

Maintaining healthy stress-beating habits, like getting plenty of exercise and taking time for exploring your creativity, can help keep you on an even keel — most of the time. Yet even the most mindful or organized person will still become distressed or overwhelmed occasionally. An argument with a friend, a boatload of school assignments all due the same day and a challenging situation at home might feel like too much to handle all at once. The suggestions in this section help you deal with those moments when, thanks to a flare-up of the stress response, you feel out of control or overwhelmed. They will give you the space you need to tamp down your temper and clear your mind.

These techniques can work for anyone, anytime. But they will work best if you've been practising stress-management techniques consistently beforehand.

25 24 23 22 21
20 19 18 17 16
15 14 13 12 11 10
9 8 7 6 5 4 3 2 1

Count Down to Calm

About to blow your top? This quick calm-down technique is as easy as one, two, three.

You count.

Go from 1 to 10, or 1 to 100. Count backwards from 25 if you prefer — it really doesn't matter.

Silent counting of any kind can help you tamp down the fight-or-flight reaction before it spins out of control. And that, in turn, will let you think more clearly and make better decisions.

Slooow Down

When you rush around in a panic, it's easy for things to go wrong. You might make clumsy, avoidable mistakes. You might miss important details. The feeling of being out of control multiplies with each misstep.

The remedy is to slow down. Even when time is short, you won't really save time by rushing. You might wind up feeling even more frazzled.

Step by Step

Breaking up your actions into small, easy steps keeps you from getting overwhelmed. It keeps you moving forward, even when you don't think you can accomplish your goal. You also get to enjoy an "I did it!" feeling of accomplishment with each successful mini advance.

> ## Take Ten
>
> Experts say taking time out for ten minutes every hour will keep you at your best without derailing you from the task at hand.

Regroup

Take a step back — literally. The physical act helps send your brain the message that you need to regroup.

During your regroup time, search for a label for your emotions. What word you come up with doesn't matter as much as the effort it takes to select one. The task distracts you just enough to short-circuit the stress response.

A time-honoured way to give yourself space to regroup is by taking a quick trip to the washroom. It offers a quiet respite where you can collect your thoughts and use your calming-down techniques in privacy.

Do a Repetitive Task

Shoot some hoops, skip rope, wash the dishes . . .

Repetitive tasks like these soothe your nervous system. They stimulate the relaxation response and quiet the mind.

They also buy you some time to sort out your emotions and come up with what your next step will be.

Apply Some Acupressure

Acupressure is a therapeutic technique based on the ancient Chinese practice of acupuncture. It involves pressing down on or squeezing specific trigger points that are found throughout your body. Each point is thought to be associated with certain emotions or body processes.

Some of the trigger points are linked to the relaxation response. By pressing these points, you may be able to help calm your nervous system during a stressful situation.

Best of all, you can do it anywhere.

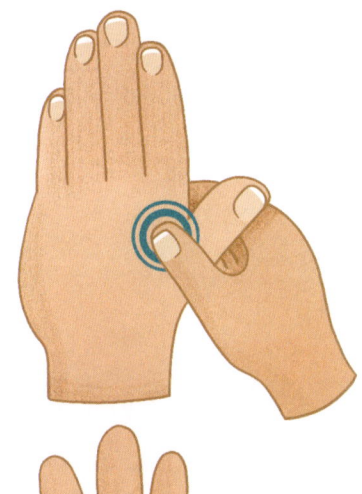

Hold out your hand, palm facing down. With the fingers of your opposite hand, press on the webbing between your thumb and pointer finger. Massage for five seconds. Focus on keeping your breath deep and slow as you press. Switch hands and repeat.

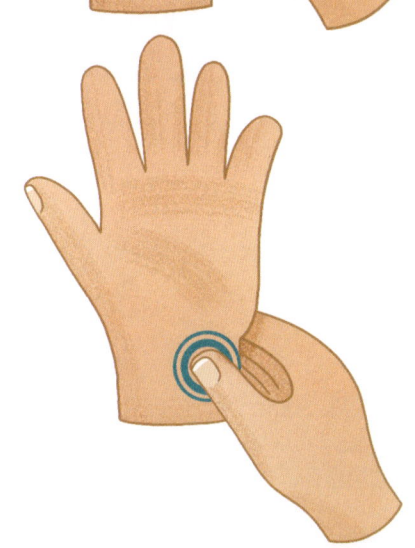

Flip your first hand over, palm facing up. Locate the acupressure point on the outer corner of your wrist. Massage it with small circular motions for a minute or two. Repeat on the opposite hand.

Shake It Off!

This active stress buster is one you might try on your washroom break. Like acupressure, it originates in an ancient Chinese healing technique. Called qigong, it involves various exercises designed to strengthen body, mind and spirit.

This exercise is called Shaking the Tree. To do it, stand with your arms at your sides. Bend your knees. When you're ready, shake it up, bounce up and down on your toes and flap your arms.

This activity will help you redirect adrenalin into movement. The shaking motions also work like a massage. A minute or two of this exercise might help you feel better able to handle the challenge awaiting you.

> **Stress Check-In**
>
> Try it now. What are you experiencing right this second as you read these words?

Picture a Rowboat

You're safe and sound, but your worries just won't stop! These strategies will help you shut down a fight-or-flight reaction triggered by your own thoughts.

Picture a rowboat tied up at a riverbank. Mentally load your worries and negative thoughts onto it. Visualize untying the boat and shoving it hard into the current. Watch the boat disappear, taking your troublesome thoughts with it.

Are you in a conflict with another person? Imagine them on the boat too!

Untangle Your Worries

What if it's not just one thing worrying you? What if it's a giant, messy tangle of stuff that has you feeling overwhelmed?

The first step, then, is to pick apart that tangle so you can examine each strand separately.

Picture your stress as a multicoloured skein of yarn. Choose one of your worries and assign it a colour, like pink. In your imaginary yarn ball, find the pink strands of yarn and pull them out. Place them in a neat pile of their own. Repeat, identifying each of your stressors and labelling them with a colour. Keep removing strands until the yarn ball is gone and you sorted all the colours into neat piles.

Doesn't that feel better already?

See Them in Their Underwear

Another popular technique for quelling nerves works particularly well when you are feeling stage fright or any kind of performance anxiety. Simply picture the members of the audience, the judge, or your adversary in nothing but their underwear! Does it make you want to laugh? That's great, because laughter helps trigger the relaxation response.

Cut Your Worries Down to Size

Now that you've separated your tangled-up emotions into clear strands, you can cut each one down to size.

On a piece of paper, write down each problem you've identified. Choose one item from your list to focus on first.

Brainstorm ways to solve this problem or reduce the stress it's causing you. If it's something like "Being late for school every day upsets me and leaves me rattled before the day begins," come up with a strategy to combat it — "I'll set my alarm fifteen minutes earlier every day." — then move on to the next item.

This activity will make you feel calmer and more in control right away. It will also help you act in positive, proactive ways that cut down your stress going forward.

Being late for school every day
- Pack my backpack before bed
- Set my alarm fifteen mins earlier

Making Decisions

Sometimes making even the smallest decisions can feel impossible. So you put it off and then feel even MORE stressed.

Stop waffling. Research shows that making a decision — any decision — relieves stress. It helps you feel better about yourself and your situation. You'll feel calmer too.

The more decisions you make, the better you'll get at it. You'll make better choices and experience fewer feelings of distress. You also feel more in control of yourself and your life.

Use these suggestions to help you make good decisions today and always.

Identify the Problem

Your first step to making a good decision is to identify the problem. That's not always easy.

Maybe you think, *I don't like school because it's boring*. But dig a little deeper and you might realize the root of the problem is not school itself, but the way you feel when kids in your class don't include you.

When you identify the real problem, you can then solve it with a good decision: Tomorrow I'll ask if I can sit with Stella and Sam during lunch.

Widen Your Circle

When you have trouble making a decision, your first instinct might be to ask friends or family for advice. That's a good idea. But the people closest to you are not the only or the best source you can tap.

You'll come up with more varied and creative ways of looking at a problem if you collect opinions from a wider, more diverse set of people. Older people, younger people, people from different backgrounds — the more the merrier.

Why? Experts say the ideas generated by people who resemble us tend to resemble ours. Someone with a different life experience might come up with a solution you and your chums might never have thought of. And it just might be the one you need right now.

So ask around for advice! The results might surprise you.

Evaluate Each Idea

Brainstorming with others helps you come up with a ton of ideas. But not all of them will be good ones!

It's time to sort them out one by one.

As you evaluate each possible course of action, ask yourself, *What might the consequences be if I choose to do this?* Imagine a few different ways the situation could play out. Do they solve your problem or make it worse?

To simplify this step, consider making a list of pros and cons. For each option, list all the good things that might result on the left side of a piece of paper, and the possible negative outcomes on the right.

You can then compare the pros and cons list for each choice. The list with the longest string of pros and a short string of cons might be your best option.

Put Off Procrastination

You've identified what's causing you stress. You've brainstormed ways to reduce or eliminate it. You've considered possible outcomes for each method. You've now arrived at the moment of decision. That can be scary!

Fear is the main reason people procrastinate, putting off a decision indefinitely. But when you procrastinate, you actually are making a decision — you're choosing to let other people guide your future.

To make sure you don't succumb to procrastination, add "do nothing" to your list of possible courses of action (page 129). Imagine different scenarios for how the future might unfold without your active input.

If doing nothing will make your situation worse, you know it's time to stop procrastinating and make a different decision.

Nothing Is Also a Choice

Sometimes doing nothing is the best decision. If so, make it a conscious choice.

Make It!

At this point, you've narrowed down your options. You've been left with a few choices that might, with a bit of luck, improve your situation and leave you less troubled and stressed.

So which do you choose? In a sense, it doesn't really matter. None of the possible decisions you make are guaranteed to work 100 percent.

That's okay, though. Making any decision — even a less-than-perfect one — is almost always better than putting it off.

First of all, you'll feel better right away. Making up your mind soothes your mind.

Second, you learn from each decision you make and improve your decision-making skills.

And third, it might actually do the trick!

It's Up to You!

There usually isn't one "correct" solution to your problem. And no one can know for sure which path is the best — except for you. Take suggestions from others, but at the end of the day, you are the one who gets to make the choice.

Sleep On It

When you're making a decision, you might hear people suggest you "sleep on it". That's good advice. While you snooze, your mind continues to evaluate your decision subconsciously. By the time your morning alarm dings, your clever brain might have found a whole new way of looking at your situation and offered up a way to tweak or change your decision for the better.

Get Your ZZZZs

You are more likely to make poor decisions when you're running on less than seven hours of sleep.

Check In with Your Emotions

Once you've made your decision, close your eyes and take a few moments to see how you feel.

A "good" decision usually leaves you feeling like a load has been taken off your shoulders. You feel happier already.

A "bad" decision might leave you feeling sick to your stomach or even more anxious than before.

Your emotions and physical reactions are important clues as to whether you're making the best possible choice for you, for right now. Don't ignore those gut feelings. Consider what they're trying to tell you and tweak your plan if you need to.

It's Okay to Change Your Mind

Here's one situation where you might want to go back on a decision: when circumstances change. For example, last night you made a decision to try out for the volleyball team today. But you just found out your favourite aunt is coming to town! Should you carry on with your plan and go to the tryout, or go home and see your auntie?

Going back on a decision is fine if it means you are taking advantage of new information. In that case, you're not actually changing your mind; you're making a new decision based on new circumstances. You might forge ahead with your original plan, but then again you may realize it's wiser to abandon ship and change course.

Press "Go"!

You put in a lot of effort identifying sources of stress, brainstorming solutions, weighing their pros and cons and coming to a sensible decision. It will come to nothing if you freeze when it's time to act. Take a deep breath, straighten your shoulders and do it.

Review the Results

An important step of decision-making takes place after the fact: reviewing your results. How well did your predictions match up with what actually happened?

If you got the results you wanted, that's great. You know your decision-making process works and you can use it again anytime you need to make a decision.

If things didn't go exactly the way you hoped they would, your review might reveal how you got derailed. You might have been overly optimistic, for example, or overlooked something important. Your review will give you critical information that will help you fine-tune your decision-making skills. You'll be able to make even better decisions going forward.

Enjoy the Afterglow

Make sure to take some time to give yourself props for making a decision and acting on it, even if it wasn't the perfect solution. Individual decisions rarely are. You'll need to keep making positive choices over and over again to get and stay less stressed.

Dealing with Conflict

Conflict, like stress, is an unavoidable part of life. There are times when people's ideas or wishes clash, and there's no way to sidestep that.

How you respond to these flashpoints can make a huge difference to your state of mind. It can even affect your physical health.

The tips in this section will help you defuse tense situations and avoid creating conflict unnecessarily.

Know the Facts

Many conflicts result from simple misunderstandings. For example, you think your sister swiped your sweater, when, in reality, you left it on the bus.

Your first step, always, is to make sure you know the facts. Instead of jumping to conclusions, ask for the other person's version of events.

The second step is to learn even more about the situation. Were other people involved? They might have different interpretations of what happened.

What about a disagreement that arises over verifiable facts? For example, what if two groups of kids are arguing in the schoolyard about which country has won the most FIFA World Cups. One group keeps shouting out it's Chile, the other insists it's Germany. There's no point letting yourself get all hot and bothered. Drop the discussion until after you've had a chance to look up the information in a book or online.

Keep Your Cool

Flying off the handle is one sure way to make any argument worse. Before you get into a kerfuffle, make sure you will be able to maintain your composure. Do some breathing exercises or blow off some steam with physical exercise to tamp down the stress response.

Present your case calmly. Keep your emotions in check and your body language relaxed. That helps the other person respond calmly too.

Take a Deep Breath

Taking a deep breath slows the release of adrenalin and tamps down the effects of cortisol. It gives your conscious mind the breathing room it needs to think more clearly about what's going on around you.

Watch Your Language

Kind, truthful and clear communication is a force for good. An overly sharp tongue or words that are confusing, angry or untrue can create tremendous harm.

You can avoid some of life's stressors simply by choosing your words carefully.

Before you sound off, ask yourself if what you're about to say is:

- true
- hurtful or unkind
- potentially offensive to the listener
- going to help you reach your goals

Depending on your answers, you might be better off holding your tongue or choosing a different approach.

Resolve the Problem

Once you are calm and have determined what a conflict is truly about, it's time to repair the rift.

Making up with an adversary should usually include these three ingredients:

- **An apology** — If you did something wrong or hurtful, intentionally or unintentionally, say you're sorry.

- **Restitution** — If you lost or damaged something that belongs to someone else, repair or replace it.

- **A plan** — Come up with a strategy for facing a similar situation in the future so you don't have the same argument over and over again.

Know When to Move On

You can't change other people's feelings. You're not responsible for them and they're not responsible for yours either. Not every conflict will end in a resolution that makes everyone equally happy. That's unfortunate but it doesn't have to take over your life.

If you can't meet each other halfway, it's probably time to move on.

How to Talk It Out

- Never attack the other person verbally or physically.
- Avoid yelling. Loud voices ramp up the tension without contributing anything new.
- Don't bring up hurts from the past.
- Use "I" statements, like "I was sad when you ripped my favourite" rather than "You ruined my hat."
- Allow the other person to "save face," even if you are 100 percent in the right.

PART 5

You've meditated and set up a daily routine. You've practised active relaxation and gone for power walks. You've tried every tip in this book.

Even so, there may be times when stress gets the better of you. This does not mean you are a failure. It just means you're human.

When you've done your best and still feel like you're in over your head, it's time to turn to others for support. Chronic stress is a real, medical condition. It can take a toll on your long-term health. There's no reason to let it continue longer than necessary, especially if you're suffering.

This section will give you guidance on how to get help.

Signs You Should Ask for Help

No one sails through life without occasionally hitting stormy seas. Even if you typically handle stress with ease, you might occasionally find yourself out of sorts. It's common, for example, when you are going through a major transition — like from elementary school to middle school — or when there are changes in your home or social life. Physical changes, like those brought on by puberty, can also add to hard-to-handle feelings of distress.

At first you might not realize that you've gone off course. Signs of distress can be sneaky. And it can be hard to admit, even to yourself, that you're not doing okay.

But it's important to recognize the signs that your everyday, normal stress has become its more harmful cousin, distress. If you are experiencing any of these warning flags, it might mean it's time to ask for help:

- Your eating patterns have changed.
- You're sleeping much more or less than usual.
- You feel overwhelmed by basic daily activities.
- You feel nervous and anxious much of the time.
- You feel sad or angry much of the time, or you feel nothing at all.
- You sometimes feel like harming yourself or others.
- You feel withdrawn or disconnected from other people.
- You have trouble concentrating.
- You have extreme mood swings.
- You feel so much distress that you feel like you can't go on.

Who Can You Ask for Help?

Your closest friends might be the first people you turn to for support. That makes sense: friends often offer good advice. They give you a shoulder to lean on. They might understand what you're going through better than anyone else.

But your friends might not have the experience or the resources to help you through tough times. Trusted adults might be better equipped to do so. They have ways to help you — like access to experts — that you and your friends don't.

Parents and other caregivers are often your first source for help. Here are some other folks you can turn to:

- A trusted relative
- Your teacher, school guidance counsellor or principal
- A sports coach
- A trusted neighbour or friend of the family
- A member of the clergy
- Your doctor or other health professional
- A Girl Guide or Scout leader, or summer camp director
- Anyone in a position of authority who you trust

How to Ask for Help

Asking for help is always hard. When you are already struggling emotionally, it can be even harder.

These simple steps can get you over the hump:

- Remind yourself that asking for help is not a sign of weakness. It's a mark of maturity and strength.
- Before you unload, ask if it's a good time. Use one of these phrases:
    - "Do you have a moment to talk?"
    - "May I ask for your advice on something that's bothering me?"
    - "I need some help. When would be a good time to talk?"
- When you have their full attention, get comfy somewhere quiet and private.
- Explain your predicament as simply as possible. Then ASK for what you think you need. Saying "I feel sad and lonely" is a good start. Following up that statement with "I would like to make new friends but don't know how" is even better.
- Don't give up. Sometimes the person you approach for help isn't the right one, or it isn't the best time for them to hear you out. Keep trying until you get the assistance you need. You deserve it.

Resources

Here are some websites, videos, books and apps where you can find more information. When using the internet, keep the following safety information in mind:

- You must be thirteen or older to use social media.
- Do not disclose your location or personal information.
- Do not agree to meet face-to-face with anyone you meet online.
- Report anything that makes you feel uncomfortable to a trusted adult.
- Everything you post online is permanent. Treat it as such.

WEBSITES

Kids Help Phone
Call this anonymous help line anytime, day or night, to get immediate, confidential assistance and advice: 1-800-668-6868.
www.KidsHelpPhone.ca

Game Changers for Mental Health
This site contains tools that were co-created by youth ambassadors and mental health professionals and educators.
www.camh.ca/en/driving-change/game-changers/game-changers-resources

Mental Health Literacy
This organization offers a "toolbox" full of resources for kids, parents and teens dealing with stress, anxiety and other mental health issues.
mentalhealthliteracy.org

Mindful
Check out Mindful for stories, meditations and mindfulness activities specifically for kids.
www.mindful.org

Nemours KidsHealth
This non-profit children's health provider maintains a top-notch website devoted to children's and teens' health.
www.kidshealth.org/en/kids/center/relax-center.html

VIDEOS

Cosmic Kids Yoga
Dozens of fun, yoga and meditation activities, especially for kids. Find them on YouTube.
www.youtube.com/c/CosmicKidsYoga

BOOKS

The Resilience Workbook for Kids: Fun CBT Activities to Help You Bounce Back from Stress and Grow from Challenges
by Caren Baruch-Feldman and Rebecca Comizio

Under Pressure : The Science of Stress
by Tanya Lloyd Kyi, illustrated by Marie-Ève Tremblay

MOBILE APPS

Breathr
Developed by the BC Children's Kelty Mental Health Resource Centre, BC Children's Centre for Mindfulness and youth, this free app provides ways to get started with mindfulness.

MindShift
Learn to relax and be mindful, develop more effective ways of thinking and use active steps to take charge of anxiety.

Mindful Powers
A free app that uses games, music, activities and more to help manage stress and practise self-calming techniques.

Smiling Mind
An app-based meditation program developed by psychologists and educators to help bring mindfulness into your life.

Index

A
Ace of Clubs, 87
acupressure, 121
adrenal glands, 8
adrenalin, 7–9, 13, 31, 52, 56, 122, 140
All the Feels!, 78
Alternate Nostril Breathing, 35
amygdala, 9
anger, 76, 77, 78
apologies, 142
Apply Some Acupressure, 121
Are You Sleepy?, 67
Are You Thirsty?, 63
Art of Giving, The, 88
asking for advice, 128
Avoid the Junk Food Trap, 62

B
Be Amazed, 49
Be A Team Player, 87
Beauty of Imperfection, The, 101
Be Flexible, 95
Be Kind to Yourself, 81
Be Willing to Bend, 29
Become a Mentor, 91
Box Breathing, 32
brain, 8–9, 48, 53, 59, 68, 70, 75, 79, 85, 86, 109, 119
brain syncing, 85
brain-to-brain synchrony, 85–86
breathing, 31, 34, 41, 106, 140
burn-out, 38, 92

C
calendars, 19, 94
Catch Some ZZZZs, 65
Celebrate Your . . . Weaknesses?, 25
cerebral cortex, 9
Changing your mind, 134
Charge Up!, 59
Check in With Your Emotions, 133
chronic stress, 13
clutter, 22, 23, 88, 106
colour coding, 21
communication, 141
complex carbohydrates, 59
conflict, 133, 138–143
conflict resolution, 123, 138–143
Conquer the Learning Curve, 28
conscious breathing, 31
Control Your Breath, 31
Cooling Breath, The, 34
Coping Strategies, 15
Corral the Clutter, 22
cortisol, 7–8, 13, 31, 56
Count Down to Calm, 117
counting, 117
Create a Vision Board, 23
creative expression, 102
creative space, 106
creativity, 102–103, 106, 110, 116
Cut Your Worries Down to Size, 125

D
daydreaming, 40
Dealing with Conflict, 138
decision making, 126, 131
de-cluttering, 22, 23, 88, 106
Deep Breathing, 41, 106, 140
distress, 7, 11, 13, 56, 126, 146
Divide to Conquer!, 21
Do a Repetitive Task, 120
Don't Flow It Alone, 104
Don't Skip Meals, 60
Draw, 112, 113
Dutch still-life paintings, 101

E
Eat a Good Breakfast, 59
eating, 58–62
emotional equilibrium, 81
emotional outbursts, 76
emotions, 72–113
endorphins, 109
Enjoy the Afterglow, 137
Enjoy the Sound of Silence, 50
epinephrine, 7
Evaluate Each Idea, 129
exercise, 45, 52–57, 68, 81, 116, 122, 140
Express Yourself, 77
eye contact, 84

F
fear, 74, 76, 130
Fight-or-flight response, 8–9, 117, 123
Fill Your Well, 103
Fine Tune the Volume, 107
finger massage, 97
flow, 102, 104–105, 109
Focus on Each Breath, 34
food, 58–62
four-square breathing, 32 (See Box Breathing)
frustration, 78

G
Get Inspired, 106
Get Organized, 18
Get Personal, 90
Get Set to Sleep, 68
Get Your ZZZZs, 132
Give More than You Get, 89
goals, 23–24, 26, 86, 91, 98, 105, 118, 141
Go with the Flow, 29, 104
gratitude journal, 80
Group Sync!, 85
Growing a Growth Mindset, 26
growth mindset, 24, 26
gut feelings, 75, 133

H
HALT, 61
hand massage, 121
Handy Reward, A, 97
happiness, 52, 74, 79, 82, 108, 133
healthy fats, 59, 61
help, getting 144–150
Home Stretch, The, 54
Home Sweet Home!, 21
hormones, 7–8, 56
   acetylcholine, 31
   adrenalin, 7–9, 13, 31, 52, 56, 122, 140
   cortisol, 7–8, 13, 31, 56
   endorphins, 109
   epinephrine, 7
   oxytocin, 84
How Not to Get Hangry, 61
How to Ask for Help, 148
How to Get Flow Going, 105
How to Improve Your Drawing and Observation Skills, 113
How to Talk It Out, 143
Hum a Tune, 108
humming, 108
hypothalamus, 9

I
Identify the Problem, 127
imagination, 103
inspiration, 106
intuition, 75
Islamic art, 101
I statements, 143
It's Okay to Change Your Mind, 134
It's Up to You!, 131

J
Jam the Circuits, 70
journaling, 15, 65, 77, 80, 110, 111
joy, 26, 44, 78, 80, 92, 109
Joy of Music!, The, 109
Jump for Joy, 80
junk food, 62
Just Add Fertilizer, 27

K
Keep a Calendar, 19
Keep a Gratitude Journal, 80
Keep a Pocket Journal, 111
Keep Your Cool, 140
Know the Facts, 139
Know When to Move On, 143
Know YOUR Stress Triggers, 13

L
Label Everything!, 21
labelling, 21–22

labyrinths, 49
Learn from the Garden, 93
Learn from the Wall, 96
learning curve, 28
Let It All Out, 56
Let It Out, 76
Listen to Your Gut, 75
Listen to Your Heartbeat, 41
Listen to Your Second Brain!, 75
list making, 26

M
Make a List!, 26
Make Beautiful Music, 109
Make It!, 131
Make It a Rainbow!, 21
Make It Aerobic, 56
Make More Eye Contact, 84
Make Space for Creativity, 106
Making Decisions, 126, 131
massage, 96–97, 121
Matter of Deep Gravity, A, 51
mazes, 49
Meditate, 45
meditation, 45, 50, 94, 103
mental health break, 81
mental synchronicity, 85
mentoring, 91
Mindful Breathing, 36
mindfulness, 44–47, 111
mindful walks, 47, 53
mindset, 24, 26
Mind Your Words, 99
Mistakes Are AMAZING!, 28
misunderstandings, 139
Mix It Up, 57
movement, 52, 122
multi-tasking, 48
music, 108, 109
Myth of Perfection, The, 100

N
napping, 67
Navajo art, 101
negative feelings, 76
nervous system, 112, 120–121
Nest It, 21
noise, 107
Nothing Is Also a Choice, 130

O
Ocean Breathing, 37
organization, 21, 22, 23
overwhelm, 116
oxytocin, 84

P
Paced Breathing, 33
Pay Back Your Sleep Debt, 66
Pay It Forward, 90
Picture a Rowboat, 123
Picture It, 39
playing an instrument, 109
positive feelings, 80
positive language, 98
positive self-talk, 98–99
Practise Clarity, 50
Practise Positive Self-Talk, 98
Press "Go"!, 135
procrastination, 80, 130
progressive relaxation, 42
proteins, 59, 61
Put a Bounce in Your Step, 53
Put Everything in Its Place, 20
Put off Procrastination, 130

Q
qigong, 122

R
random acts of kindness, 90
Regroup, 119
relaxation response, the, 30–31, 31, 52, 108, 112, 121, 144
repetitive tasks, 120
Reserve Judgment, 78
resolution, 142
Resolve the Problem, 142
rest, 64–71
restitution, 142
Review the Results, 136
rewards, 96–97, 104
Reward Yourself, 96
routines, 94–95

S
sadness, 10, 74, 76–77, 146
Say it in Person, 83
Say No to Multi-tasking, 48
second brain, The, 75
See Them in their Underwear, 124
self-care, 92–94, 102
Self-Care Triangle, The, 93
self-massage, 96–97
Shake It Off!, 122
shaking the tree, 122
Share Your Feelings, 83
Signs You Should Ask for Help, 146
silence, 50, 107
silent retreats, 50
singing, 109
sitali pranayama, 34
sleep, 64–71
sleep debt, 66
sleep deficit, 66
sleep journal, 65
Sleep On It, 132
Slooow Down, 118
Snack Attack!, 60
social networks, 73, 82
So Many Feelings!, 77
spirit lines, 101
Stand in Tree Pose, 43
Start Fresh, 71

Stay in the Moment, 46
Step by Step, 118
Stick to a Routine, 94
Stifling feeling, 76
Stress Check In, 123
stressors, 12–13, 18, 124
stress reactions, 10–11, 14
stress response, 8, 12, 115–116, 119, 140
stretching, 45, 54, 81
suppressing feelings, 77
Switch Up Your Routine, 68
Synchronize Your Brain with Someone Else's, 85

T
Take a Deep Breath, 140
Take a Mindful Walk, 47
Take a Nap, 67
Take a Shower, 107
Take a Stress Self-Check, 11
Take Regular Mental Health Breaks, 81
Take Ten, 119
Take Time to Daydream, 40
Talk Yourself through It, 99
team sports, 86
Team Up, 86
tension sources, 11
Think Function First!, 21
Think Vertically!, 21
thirst, 63
thought-seeds, 26
Too MUCH Stress!, 12
tree pose, 43 (See Yoga)
Try Progressive Relaxation, 42
Turn a New Page, 71
Tweak Your Routine, 95

U
Untangle Your Worries, 124

V
Visibility is Key!, 21
vision boards, 23
Visit Your Happy Place, 79
visualization, 11, 39, 79, 123

W
wabi-sabi, 101
Watch Your Language, 141
When to Look Away, 84
Who Can You Ask for Help?, 147
Widen Your Circle, 128
Write Down Your Worries, 69
Write in a Journal, 110

Y
yoga, 34, 68

Z
zone, the, 104, 105, 112